Early Praise for
The Building Trust 60-Day Workout

"In **The Building Trust 60-Day Workout,** you'll learn many important lessons, and like any workout, it won't be easy, and it won't be quick. But Bruce's own experiences and vulnerability shed light on just about any situation you could find yourself in, and he shares practical insights to help build trusting relationships at home or at work. You'll want to refer back to this book again and again."

Paul Spiegelman
Entrepreneur, Author, and Co-Founder, Small Giants Community

"Wisdom doesn't come quickly. **The Building Trust 60-Day Workout** is a daily devotional where each page explores a profound insight on the slow process of learning to build trust at home, work, and in your community. Bruce has been teaching and thinking deeply about this topic for a long time. His humble wisdom and good humor shine through this book as the pragmatic meditation of a seasoned leader.

I wouldn't suggest skimming through the pages to get a sense of Bruce's message. Sure, you can do it, but it will be like flying by amazing works of art. The value is in the reflection. What does this say to me? Have I encountered a similar situation? How did I fall short? How might I be a better human?

I especially liked the meditation on the cost of mistrust. Business leaders who fail to build trust don't see the missed opportunities and costs they incur. Wasted time, lost productivity, employee and customer turnover, poor health carry a cumulative burden. As Bruce recommends, take steps today to counter mistrust, even if the outcomes aren't visible overnight. Read this book, slowly, thoughtfully."

Ty Hagler
Principal, Trig

"I have been a business leader for over twenty years, and continue to be challenged to be better through Bruce's inspirational words and Building Trust resources. We are a healthier organization because many staff members have attended Bruce's two-day workshops. We still need to continually practice true vulnerability in building stronger relationships throughout our organization, and I am excited to share Bruce's new book **The Building Trust 60-Day Workout** with my staff."

Judy Talcott
President & CEO, Goodwill Industries of Wayne & Holmes Counties, Inc.

"I appreciate Bruce's focus on taking personal responsibility for our relationships and the level of trust attained. He makes it clear that trust is ultimately about being trustworthy and valuing others. This isn't just true for sixty days, but should be applied daily as a lifelong exercise regime. Bruce presents this in an engaging, down-to-earth, and extremely practical way. He demonstrates the humility necessary to build trust that lasts.

One comes away from reading **The Building Trust 60-Day Workout** with a knowledge that humility, self-awareness, and honesty with ourselves and others is essential to being trustworthy and building trusting relationships. Whether in our vocation, relationships or family, we all have influence. Influence flows out of character, and a foundational aspect of character *is trustworthiness. Bruce's book and insights have emphasized this in a unique and very beneficial way."*

Joel Montgomery, PE, MSM, ICMA-CM
Director of Administration/City Manager
City of Wooster, Ohio

---

*"The **Building Trust 60-Day Workout** demonstrates what an architect and master builder of trust Bruce Hendrick is. Through a concise, easy to understand blueprint, it is designed to help us strengthen our trust muscles."*

Brian E. Krebs
Attorney

---

*"As an entrepreneur for over 25 years, I've learned that trust as a foundation determines the health of our team. This is one of the many reasons I love Bruce and his book. **The Building Trust 60-Day Workout** is practical, thought-provoking, and action-oriented. It's a book we will use at imageOne to help reinforce and enhance our culture."*

Rob Dube
President, imageOne: Forbes 25 Best Small Company in America; Ranked the #1 Top Workplace in Michigan
Author of the book **donothing,** the most rewarding leadership challenge you will ever take

*"**The Building Trust 60-Day Workout** is a daily guide for building more meaningful relationships in your personal and/or work life and focuses on what works in the real world. Each day emphasizes a specific topic for building trust, describes real world examples on that topic and challenges you with a call for action. This is an easy read that I find myself picking up over and over again to reinforce what I can do to build more trust and connect with others, especially in challenging relationships."*

Rhonda Billman
Assistant Director, Wooster Campus of The Ohio State University, CFAES

"As Bruce would remind us all: building trust requires showing trust. The first day on my new job leading RBB (Bruce's electronic manufacturing business), I walked into his office and written in large letters on his whiteboard was, 'I don't know, have you asked Jim yet?' This was not an abdication of his authority, but a bold statement of his trust in me. He demonstrated his passion for building trust with no uncertainty."

Jim Tennant
Former President, RBB

The Building Trust 60-Day Workout

Also by Bruce Hendrick

On My Own: Recollections of an Unlikely CEO

The Building Trust 60-Day Workout

*Powerful Daily Lessons Proven
to Build Trust at Work and at Home*

BruceHendrick
BUILDING TRUST

TRUST HOUSE
PUBLISHING

A Trust Enterprises Company

Wooster, Ohio

The Building Trust 60-Day Workout:
Powerful Daily Lessons Proven to Build Trust at Work and at Home
© 2019, Bruce Hendrick. All Rights Reserved.
Trust House Publishing, Wooster, Ohio

978-1-7340489-0-2 (paperback)
978-1-7340489-1-9 (eBook)
Library of Congress Control Number: 2019914159

brucehendrick.com | 330-601-0898

Publishing consultant: David Wogahn, AuthorImprints.com

TABLE OF CONTENTS

"Few delights can equal the mere presence
of one whom we trust utterly."
—**George MacDonald,** Scottish author,
poet, and Christian minister

"If you are untrustworthy,
people will not trust you."
—**Lao Tzu**, ancient Chinese
philosopher and writer

FOREWORD

Trust is the lifeblood of business culture, as any student of organizational dynamics can tell you. Without it, companies are racked with problems that can all be traced back to the same source, namely, the dysfunction created whenever employees don't trust their leadership, their organization, or each other. In Patrick Lencioni's classic *The Five Dysfunctions of a Team,* "absence of trust" is the first and most important dysfunction and is the source of all the other dysfunctions.

On the other hand, companies with strong bonds of trust tend to get recognized sooner or later as great places to work. Indeed, trust is explicitly what the Great Place to Work institute seeks to measure in judging the quality of a company's culture. The measuring tool it uses is its well-known (and trusted) survey called the Trust Index.

That said, trust is won or lost on different levels and in different ways. There is, to begin with, trust between individuals, which is the focus of this eminently readable and practical guide to trust-building by Bruce Hendrick. In organizations, however, some individuals—namely leaders—have influence that goes well beyond their one-on-one relationships with other individuals. A leader's primary responsibility is to establish trust with the led, which among other things involves creating a general climate of trust in the organization, unit, or team.

A good example is Edward Jones, the $8-billion, century-old investment advisory firm, which in 2019 marked its 20th year on *Fortune*'s list of Best Places to Work. Under managing partner (that is, chief executive) Jim Weddle, it actively promoted what Ed Frauenheim—Director of Research and Content at Great Place to Work—calls a For All Trust Mindset, defined as "a belief that all your people are capable of generating good ideas, are well-intentioned, and are vital to include to improve processes and products." Penny Pennington, who succeeded Weddle in January 2019, has thought just as deeply about the trust-leadership connection. "Trust can never be claimed," she says. "It can only be earned. That happens through the making and keeping of promises, which is actually the core of commerce."

In a corporate setting, there is one other critical trust relationship to consider—namely, that between individuals and the organization as a whole. No matter how much leaders do to promote trust, they can only get so far if the company's finances are hidden from employees. Without knowledge of the finances, people can't know how secure their jobs are, or what they can do to enhance their job security and help the company achieve its goals.

Traditionally, of course, thinking about such matters has been the province of top executives who would then come up with the tasks and objectives that managers and employees were expected to carry out. It's a system patterned after the military and commonly referred to as "command and control." Some companies, however, have experimented with an entirely different way of operating based on the same premise that Jim Weddle used at Edward Jones—namely, that employees are well-intentioned and will gladly do whatever the organization needs, assuming they know what it is. Management's responsibility is to provide the information and training the employees need and then trust them to do the best they can, while keeping an eye on what they're doing to make sure they get it right. This approach is perhaps best characterized as "trust and track" (in contrast to "command and control"), and a prime example is open-book management, particularly the system I wrote about with Jack Stack, its originator, in *The Great Game of Business.*

For those dealing with a trust issue right now—and I suspect you are or you wouldn't be here—you've come to the right place. You can't read *The Building Trust 60-Day Workout* without thinking about all of the factors that have gone into creating whatever untrusting relationships you have had, or continue to have, especially those for which you may bear some responsibility. Bruce Hendrick offers sound advice and a solid program that will teach you as much about yourself as about the relationships you're struggling with. You will come out a better person on the other side.

—**Bo Burlingham,** author of
Small Giants and *Finish Big*

ACKNOWLEDGMENTS

This book is dedicated to my authentic and trustworthy children: Kelly, Kara, and Kirk. Each of you expects constructive and real conversations with me and each other. As a result, we have honest, accepting, and loving relationships based on how things are, not as we would have them. You helped me shape the content of this workout, sometimes knowingly, sometimes through trial and error. Thanks, guys! I appreciate our peaceful and trusting connections more than you know.

To the countless **Building Trust Experience** workshop clients whom I've had the privilege of serving through the years, thank you for your willingness to become vulnerable. You have helped to hone the concepts in this book, one gutsy issue at a time. By expecting more from your work lives and relationships, you've dismantled your own barriers both to earning and extending trust. My hat's off to you for doing this—frequently in the presence of strangers.

I owe my deepest gratitude to my many bosses, coworkers, friends, church members, and fellow volunteers who've shown me time and again how *universal* the building trust concepts are. Thank you for sharing your journeys with me.

Special thanks to my daughter Kelly for her editing services! Grammatical errors remaining in the text were no doubt caught by Kelly and overridden by me.

Finally, this book is available in its handy format through the inspired administration and unwavering support of Carrie Guenther, Trust Ambassador at Building Trust, LLC. Without Carrie, this book would be (another?) one of my someday ideas. Thanks and bravo, Carrie!

Bruce Hendrick
Founder and President, Building Trust, LLC
CEO and Owner, RBB

INTRODUCTION

Much of the interpersonal, family, and team dysfunction that I've witnessed throughout the years has been caused by a lack of trust between members. If your goals depend on other people and you struggle accomplishing them, this book will arm you with many practical approaches to get unstuck.

I've also lived the thrill of building many teams and coaching countless others to achieve high levels of mutual trust. The unity, mojo, and performance that arises when members trust each other is joyous. In such an environment, we can be ourselves, count on each other, and constructively deal with shared challenges with a fraction of the typical stress.

This book was written on the eleventh anniversary of the founding of Building Trust, LLC, and is based on a lifetime of in-the-trenches experience with these issues. I grew up in a family environment that was challenged by severe and persistent mental illness, an environment which offered precious little day-to-day trust. (For the complete story, read *On My Own, Recollections of an Unlikely CEO.*)

I've had two wives and raised three children. I've worked in a myriad of professional environments: thirteen years in corporate America, three years in a five-generation family business, and nineteen years in a small private company. I've also been a part of two business startups and countless volunteer organizations.

I've taken part in teams of all stripes: organized sports, scouting, off-shift manufacturing, middle management, executive leadership, peer advisory groups, church leadership councils, boards of directors, 12-step programs, and multiple overseas missions. I've learned that while people's backgrounds and circumstances vary widely, there are some fundamental truths at the root of earning trust.

By paying close attention to what succeeds, and what doesn't, I've been able to share with audiences across America the practical side of trust-building, and now I'm sharing it with you. In the pages ahead, I invite you to join me as we travel the highly rewarding road of building trust, one day at a time.

For the purposes of this book, let's define trust as the *feeling* that one person has for another of confidence, predictability, and, when needed, personal support. Trust is built one relationship at a time. It varies from complete trust to utter distrust. We rarely bestow our trust to groups of people—we trust individuals or we don't.

WHY THIS BOOK EXISTS

Okay, but why write this book? Why should you, the reader, actively build trust?

First, too many teams of highly talented and dedicated people hit a wall of frustration and performance because they are stuck in what appear to be intractable problems when the actual root cause is mistrust among the members. When safety is lacking, people withhold information and opinions, posturing becomes routine, and mediocrity abounds. Once safety is restored, it's like a logjam breaks; the team rediscovers its latent energy to meet its challenges. I've assisted many groups through this difficulty by applying the lessons included in this book, and this book is my opportunity to share the wealth.

Second, it's been my experience that some great people have blind spots on the impact we have on our work and home relationships. We sow seeds of mistrust without even knowing it, label others as untrustworthy, and then react accordingly. Throughout these sixty lessons, I hope to flip on the light switch so we can see what we're actually doing with, and to, those around us.

Finally, I aim for the reader to share in the pure joy that comes with genuine trust. There is nothing quite like it. Love is wonderful, but love is not required to build trust. To fully trust another person is the height of vulnerability and security, while to have earned another person's trust is a great honor and rare privilege. To be trusted is to be accepted— and respected—as the unique person you are. Does it get any better?

So I welcome you to this workout for building trust in your relationships. This book is designed for you if:

- You know that trust matters and want a practical resource to make it happen,
- You want more meaningful and free-flowing connections with others in your life,
- You are tired of waiting for others to build or restore your trust in them,
- You want to know why some people press your *do not trust* button, and when you might be pressing theirs,
- You have had enough theory; it's time for specific, practical, and proven strategies and actions,

- You are open-minded and willing to extend trust to others *under the right circumstances,* and

- You are ready to commit yourself, as with any workout, to make changes.

This book is not for you if you believe the amount of trust in your life is other people's responsibility.

THE FORMAT

Every day, a different element of trust-building is presented. Since the audience is anyone who wants to build more trust in their lives, the examples draw from both life and workplace settings. Avoiding clichés and complex theories, I share what works *in the real world,* in bite-sized chunks.

Why the sixty-day format? Because while mistrust can be created by one incident (or even one moment), trust is most often built over an extended period. I hope to encourage you every step of the way. After two months, you will have experienced a comprehensive introduction into what is needed to be a successful trust-builder. You will better understand your strengths and improvement opportunities in this arena.

HOW TO READ THIS BOOK

There are four great ways to consume the material in this book. You can:

1. Use it as a daily reflection and meditation, pausing to give each day an intentional focus
2. Do the above but weekly instead of daily, to allow for deeper, more substantial change in yourself and relationships
3. Do a quick read-through to capture the main concepts, and then focus on your selected interest areas
4. Use it as a handy reference by employing the Topic Index (in the back).

CLEAR YOUR MIND BEFORE WE BEGIN

Note 1: I confess to making every mistake in the area of building trust. Some of my important relationships have failed because of trust problems in one direction or the other, or both. And I'm in good company. Otherwise, you wouldn't have picked up this book. As you read these pages, I encourage you to let the past stay there.

Note 2: Others don't magically become trustworthy just because we want to build trust. Yes: knuckleheads (and worse) abound. You've been burned by humans before. Alas, this book won't prevent future disappointment. Your brain is on danger alert, even when you aren't aware of it, so this book will never encourage you to ignore your instincts. They're valid and essential. Okay? Good.

Note 3: But let's make a deal right now: we will leave others to be responsible for themselves so we can approach each day focused on *how to get off other people's Do Not Trust list.* This, after all, is up to us.

No one works each concept in this book perfectly; happily, there's no need. Part of trusting another human being is the opportunity to be our flawed selves along the way. Sincere effort is often enough.

Do only what you can each day. Try again tomorrow from a slightly different angle. Over time, others around you will notice a profound difference in your trustworthiness. They will learn to rely on you, confide in you, and join you in your efforts. And you will be rewarded by feeling more comfortable to do the same with them.

DAY 1: READY TO TRUST?

Three frogs sat on a log. One decided to jump off. How many were left? Three! Deciding isn't the same as jumping.

An old Chinese proverb states: *The best time to plant a tree is twenty years ago. The second-best time is now.* It'd be nice if we already had many mutually trusting relationships and the ability to form new ones at will. But if we look at our most challenging interactions, we see that it's primarily up to us to plant the trees.

Building trust is hard work. It takes a conscious choice backed by purposeful action. Are we ready? Here's a favorite movie scene to consider:

Mr. Miyagi:	*Now, ready?*
Daniel:	*Yeah, I guess so.*
Miyagi:	[Sigh] *Daniel-san, must talk.*
[both kneel]	
Miyagi:	*Walk on road, hmm? Walk left side, safe. Walk right side,*

safe. Walk middle, sooner or later [makes squish gesture] *get squish, just like grape.*

Here, karate, same thing. Either you karate do "yes" or karate do "no." You karate do "guess so," [makes squish gesture]—*just like grape. Understand?*

Daniel: *Yeah, I understand.*

Miyagi: *Now, ready?*

Daniel: *Yeah, I'm ready.*

The Karate Kid (1984), Columbia Pictures, written by Robert Mark Kamen

So, I humbly ask again, are we ready?

The time for waiting is over. Today I acknowledge that I have much to learn to actively earn someone's trust. I will keep my eyes open for opportunities, paying particular attention to relationships that aren't functioning well today.

DAY 2: IT STARTS HERE

L et's think of someone we distrust; picturing a name and face helps a lot. Experience tells us that, deep down, we don't like them very much. We wonder if they tell the truth. We lock onto points of disagreement to keep that person at arm's length. We see their humanity and hold it against them. Their opinion of us is not that important. We don't go the extra mile, and often not even the standard ones. Little if any gut-level honesty is shared in either direction. The relationship feels like staged and pointless choreography. If we can manage it, we avoid the person altogether.

Now let's picture a person we fully trust. It can be a sibling, spouse, coworker, friend, parent, pastor, coach, whomever. If choosing a trusted face comes slowly, no worries—it's not uncommon.

What can we say about this person? We like them as people. We believe what they say. We respect their opinion, even when it differs from ours. We see their humanity and forgive them. We don't want to disappoint them. We want them to trust us in return—so we behave more trust*worthy*. When we work with them, we likely give our best effort. We can be ourselves; this relationship feels free-flowing, easy, and natural. They level with us for our own good, and we want to hear it!

This strong relationship took time to grow. And in the real world, surrounded by humans, let's not pretend that we can somehow convert our distrust into fully trusting relationships solely with decent skills and techniques. It takes two.

And let's also admit this: there are people in our lives—our family and friends, our church, our workplace, and our community—who don't include us on their fully-trusted list. Since we want more trust, and we can't change other people, it follows that the change we're looking for has to start in the mirror.

I want to be my true self, to be at my best, and to increase my influence in the world. Since I can't make others trustworthy, the way to expand trust is to actively and consciously build it myself. Today I will pick a specific person I trust and write down a list of reasons why I think I trust them.

DAY 3: I'M SORRY

One of the best things we can do today to restore trust in a broken or damaged relationship is to apologize—not like we were forced to as children—but sincerely, humbly, and with genuine concern for the other person we may have hurt.

Remember, there is no need to grovel; we just need to own our behavior, without blame or excuse, and without the expectation of their forgiveness—or even a response at all. "I'm sorry, can I try that again?" or "I apologize; that wasn't my best me."

Is there someone at work, in our family, or in our circle of friends that is due an apology from us today? Have we been self-justifying our problematic behavior instead of seeking to build harmony and strength in the relationship? Do we secretly hope we don't run into this person today? Are we operating under the assumption that it's better to appear right than to look weak or mistaken? If so, perhaps we've lost sight of our goal: a strong, mutually trusting relationship.

A sincere apology is a trust deposit. It validates the other person as someone worthy of our caring, respect, and time. "I'm sorry" feels good to them and it relieves us of the burden we carry. And once our façade of perfection lifts, trust has room to grow once again.

On the flipside, mistrust accumulates quickly. Each day that goes by while someone waits for an apology is another day of trust erosion.

On this day I acknowledge the price I pay for declining to apologize. I'll summon the courage to admit my humanity and break free from a worse problem down the road. I know that trust requires vulnerability. Today, it starts with me, so I'll find someone and make a sincere apology.

DAY 4: THE TRUST HACK

Sorry, there is no shortcut to building trust. A baby develops in nine months; some things take time.

Trust can't be rushed. In fact, a person with the goal of accelerating trust is often not to be trusted, right? (They must have some agenda.) No, if we're in a hurry to accomplish something, the best thing to do is just say so, openly. This way at least our transparency will count in our favor.

The pace of any relationship is set by the willingness of both persons to extend trust, not to earn it. We can do a lot to set the stage for healthy trust; these techniques are highlighted elsewhere in this book. But we must always remember that someone else's propensity to trust has been shaped by a lifetime of experiences and people that came along well before we did.

Trust takes as long as it takes. Even if we do everything right (and we won't). Even if we're the most trustworthy person on the planet, the other person may have lived a history of disappointments, broken promises, and betrayals. So it's important to persevere and to avoid taking our inevitable bumps along the trust road personally.

New friends, romantic partners, supervisors, and pastors all yearn to be trusted right away. Since we can't force it to happen, let's use this time to our advantage. Let's try to relate: do we struggle trusting people and, if so, is this based on their recent actions or our past history?

While waiting, let's be as open (Day 13, *Transparency*) and accountable (Day 9, *Good Intentions*) as we can be.

Today I will give another person the time and emotional space they need to trust me. Meanwhile, I will work on becoming more trustworthy, should that time ever arrive.

DAY 5: JUST SAY IT

Many of us tend to sit back and allow others to talk or ask a question rather than give our opinion or offer a solution. We hesitate over whether our position or experience is enough to merit sharing our views. Then, once again, we spend the car ride home reliving the discussion in our minds, mentally kicking ourselves for what we *should* have said.

This is quite familiar to those of us who are patient, attentive listeners. We've gained friends, influence, and a certain amount of self-worth through letting others be heard—and this is a great thing!

But how many times do we look like we are listening but are, in fact, formulating our response *just so*? Or calming our emotional reaction to what's been said? Or waiting for the perfect time to jump in? Or deciding whether we can trust the other person with our honest opinion? Or fearing to cause a passionate outburst?

And so we don't engage, and another opportunity to connect with others slips past. This isolation can be frustrating, especially since others seem to glide through difficult subjects with ease. To change things, we need more effective self-talk.

As small children, we knew how to get our needs met (ask any mom). We didn't need the right words or that particular moment in time. We just said it. As adults, when the discomfort of *not* getting our needs met is strong enough to overcome our silence, we will talk.

We need some new internal dialog. We know we are polite; we need not fear giving offense. We can speak our minds with caring and respect. Right now is the best (and perhaps only) opportunity to speak up. We're not responsible for how others react to our opinions.

On this day, for the sake of team trust, I will share what I really think. I don't want to relive today's conversations later on. It's game time.

DAY 6: GOING SOMEWHERE

Building trust requires a conscious, ongoing effort. The workout in this book prepares you by creating a full awareness of what it takes. Daily practice creates muscle memory, so it becomes a natural way of operating. But if we desire to build trust into a relationship that isn't going anywhere, none of this understanding much matters.

This relationship needs a common goal to achieve something meaningful, together. A key and powerful trust-building tool is *work itself*. When people work together to accomplish a worthwhile mutual goal, trust has a much higher chance to develop. The goal itself is not the point; any clear target will do, as long as it requires shoulder-to-shoulder interdependence to make it happen.

Combining efforts with another person, usually under the pressure of achieving results, and often with a deadline, creates an environment that tests and stretches trust. Can I count on this person? Are they reliable? Do they care about me? Do they dig deep and give more of themselves when the pressure is on? Am I as trustworthy as the other person needs me to be? These questions and many more can best be answered when something *important* is on the line.

The absence of significant, shared objectives relieves the pressure. It permits both players to drop into safe (non-vulnerable) mode, which hits the brakes on trust.

So as part of our trust-building regimen, we want to commit to something with the other person. For example: plan an event, work on a big project, re-establish peace in the family, or support a cause in the community. Tackling a jointly valued project can be a great platform for the relationship. It helps to rewrite the stories in our heads by revealing the underlying value in the other person.

To build trust today, I will do something meaningful with another person. Each of us will then have a better chance to earn trust from the other.

DAY 7: UNTEACHABLE

We can overcome our own lack of trust by facing our fears or letting others earn our confidence, but that choice can't be imposed upon us. We simply do or do not trust certain people or situations. Others can't convince us to the contrary. Our trusting "switch" is deep down in our limbic (primal) brains.

Anyone who's adopted a rescue animal can attest to this. Our new pet doesn't know that we're trustworthy or have their best interests at heart. Whatever caused their mistrust or fear has sunk deep, where the current evidence doesn't reach. It may take weeks, months, or years for our companion to trust us completely, let alone our friends and family. Rescues only overcome their earlier (often unknown) traumas with patience, love, and a lot of repetitive trust-building from us.

In my experience, people aren't much different. The limbic brain is commanding, automatic, and subconscious. Put me on a high bridge over water and, despite reason and evidence, my hands sweat, my pulse races, and my neocortex (thinking brain) goes offline. Likewise, specific people can trigger unsafe feelings; we just don't trust them. Unlike pets, however, we humans learn to hide our emotions well.

It's why this book focuses on trust-building, not on trusting. I assume that the reader is already trust-*worthy* and has good intentions. We are developing our own toolbox to become more easily trusted by others while maintaining reasonable expectations as well. We are here to learn to demonstrate, through our consistent long-term behaviors, that we are safe. This workout will help us stay aware of what we're doing and become competent in its application.

Today I appreciate that I don't know the traumas others have faced along the way, so I don't know how readily they can trust me. It's okay; I won't take it personally. I will keep the dialog open and stay patient.

DAY 8: BE YOURSELF

Trust is only built with genuine people. Most of us can easily spot a phony person, and our emotional walls go up automatically. We begin to feel manipulated as if we're being led along for a hidden purpose. As a result, we pull away, often carefully disguising our uneasiness.

There are lots of reasons why people cover their thoughts and feelings: introversion, natural shyness, general mistrust, outright fear, etc. In many families and cultures, acting in a guarded way can even be the norm. We pick up nonverbal signals of caution right away and involuntarily respond in kind. Guardedness has its place in life, but when trying to build trust, it gets in our way.

It follows, then, that if we expect others to trust us, we need to be our true selves. Acting out-of-character to impress someone might work, but our authentic self will eventually show up, and when it does, the trust we thought we earned slips away.

Think about it: when someone trusts a *version* of us, it's just a mirage anyway.

Now, consider. When we interact with someone we fully trust, do we worry about sharing what's on our mind? Or how it comes out? No, probably not. And that's the real beauty of trust; we can be ourselves, unfiltered. Genuine trust abides no half-truths or partial disclosures.

As we go about our day, let's be watchful for whether we're packaging our thoughts to manage or control another person's reaction. When trust exists, there is lightness and ease to our communication, where unpleasant topics are discussed almost as freely as pleasant ones.

Today, I choose to leave my masks at home. I express my real self to the people around me so my relationships can grow deep roots.

DAY 9: GOOD INTENTIONS

"Do or do not. There is no try." Master Yoda, *Star Wars,* 1977

Busy, ambitious people make lots of promises. When we commit, we honestly intend to follow through. We mean well. Of course we do. But things change sometimes. At times it's out of our control. You understand, I'm sure.

Full stop! This is how the habitual apologizer self-justifies. Frequent confessions for missed commitments spoil trust and reflect poor self-discipline. It's time to get real: trust is earned when we see things through, not by "trying." We must learn to make only those commitments that we hold ourselves accountable to keep.

This is easy to illustrate. When people fail to keep a commitment to you, do you remember it? Do you always let them know? Are you more suspicious the next time they promise something? The more we want to trust someone, the more these issues matter.

We watch for patterns. Fair or unfair, we draw conclusions as to their reliability.

So whether or not others confront us about it, let's not kid ourselves; people around us pay attention to our commitment performance. Few things can destroy trust more quickly than a pattern of broken promises. It's much better to face the consequences of saying "no" up-front than to miss a commitment. Trust-builders treat their word as the obligation it really is.

We might say, "I can see how important this is to you, but I value our relationship too much to promise what I can't deliver." Operating in this manner builds trust in four ways: it's the truth, it builds credibility, it limits promises to only those we expect to keep, and it shortens our list!

Today, I will take extra care not to over-commit. To whatever I agree to accomplish, I hold myself accountable, without excuse.

DAY 10: SEIZE THE DAY

No one enjoys conflict. If we have a problem with another person and simply hope the mounting struggle will get easier, we are in for a long wait. Small troubles tend to grow and potentially disrupt the relationship or business at hand.

Yes, we do need to choose our battles. But most of us know which issues need to be dealt with, and we often choose otherwise. An unaddressed problem is much like holding a beach ball under the water; it takes more effort to keep the ball submerged (and pretend the issue is insignificant) than to let it surface and handle it.

When unresolved interpersonal tensions go on for an extended period, one or both parties can decide the relationship is not worth additional investment. Dialog drops into gracious sweetness or fades altogether. Free and easy trust gets replaced with the familiar "we have to work together" attitude. This is what happens when the day is not seized!

We know we are building trust when we feel safe enough to privately discuss challenging subjects in spite of any short-term awkwardness. As usual, it starts with us.

Just for today, I refuse to let my fear of conflict morph into accumulated stress. To keep my relationships fresh and growing, I seize the opportunity and wade through my difficulties as soon as they emerge, despite my momentary discomfort.

DAY 11: HONORING OTHERS

There is no greater honor than to give someone our full attention, listen for deep understanding, and choose to be influenced by what they say.

Do we listen with the *intent* to be persuaded? Are we sincerely interested in learning the nuances and complexities of the other person's viewpoint? Or do we more often look for weakness in their position? Most of us prepare counterarguments while others are still talking: "Yeah, but... !"

In these days of polarized rhetoric and divisive online posts, traditional concepts like statesmanship and mutual respect have lost some luster. When we are utterly convinced of our rightness, there is scarce room for alternative views and, therefore, little reason for deep listening.

Put another way: if our interactions are mainly competitive disagreements, trust suffers. Contempt and dishonor are not far behind.

Here's the thing: if you don't listen to me, I assume you don't care much about what's going on in my head and so I figure you don't care about me as a person. And if you don't care about me, I can't afford to trust you (See Day 17, *Value Others*).

Trust is built best when both parties speak, listen, and have equal chances of influencing the end results.

Today, I will do someone the honor of being fully present to their experience, ideas, and perspective. Who knows? Maybe tomorrow they will listen to my own.

DAY 12: BLIND TRUST

Trust is a two-way street. It requires trust-*worthiness* from the trust-ed and trust-*willingness* from the trust-er. We've all learned, usually the hard way, that not everyone is worthy of our trust. Getting let down by fellow human beings is a part of life. And while occasional shortcomings come with being human, patterns of unreliability should not be disregarded.

Those who easily and rapidly extend trust to others are a breath of fresh air. This willingness to trust another person—to give someone the benefit of the doubt—is a terrific quality and half the trust battle. But when this trust-willingness turns into blind (careless) trust, high-risk lurks.

Three consistent behavior patterns indicate whether our trust in another person is well-founded: communication, competency, and personal caring. Let's keep our eyes open by asking ourselves:

- How has communication been recently? Is it honest and open? Can I level with this person? Do I feel like I know what's really going on?
- Do I feel in the loop? When I ask questions, do I get the same quality of answers as when the relationship was new?
- Can I count on them to follow through? Will it be on time and as promised?
- When they fall behind or don't know how to do something, do they get help?
- Does this person offer repeated apologies, excuses, and/or renegotiations?
- Do I sense that the person cares about me as an individual? Do they spare any time for me?

No one is perfect, so it's best to set reasonable expectations. Everyone has bad days. However, if we're frequently surprised or disappointed and we grow uneasy, our gut is telling us something we should not ignore!

Today, I will keep my eyes open. The trust I place in others is a valuable gift; I choose wisely those who receive it.

DAY 13: TRANSPARENCY

Openness and vulnerability allow the light to shine in relationships. Fear, defensiveness, and closed minds offer only darkness. Transparency encourages trust because we relate better to those who show they are flawed and human—people similar to ourselves.

This is not to say that to build trust we must reveal our every thought and belief. We're entitled to our private opinions and feelings; it's part of what keeps us mentally and emotionally healthy. Still, let's keep in mind what the research says: unless there are very high levels of trust already, in the absence of information, most people fill the voids with *negative assumptions*. In other words, if we stay silent about something, it's unwise to presume that we are being given the benefit of the doubt.

Trust grows when we take risk—and in no other way. Without some level of exposure, others can't earn our confidence. As we lower our walls, we give others the chance to prove they can respond appropriately. The more they can handle, the more of our private thoughts we can share, and pretty soon we feel safer.

Conversely, great opportunities arise when others get candid with us. By rolling with the conversation, not taking difficult matters personally, and limiting our fight-or-flight response, we can inspire others to share the real deal.

Overly polite and guarded conversations reveal little and offer few chances to earn trust. Walls, in any form, impede the trust we are trying to develop.

Today, I will err on the side of transparency and openness; I will let someone know me. Even with baby steps, I can learn to expand my sphere of safety. If someone honors me today with their direct and candid opinion, I will treat it like the gift it is.

DAY 14: VICTIMS AND VILLAINS

We are not victims. Others are not villains. This kind of thinking kills the opportunity to build trust. It robs us of our available choices and keeps us stuck. No one is truly helpless. Instead, we might ask ourselves what we can do to further our objective—and then go do that.

While we recognize humankind's capacity for inflicting harm, intentionally or otherwise, we also know that focusing on others' misdeeds and omissions gives us a ready excuse to admit defeat. We are entitled to appropriate protection and self-care, but if this comes at the price of our ongoing misery, are we any better off?

Seeing others as villains, seeing ourselves as victims, and/or giving in to self-imposed helplessness torpedoes any real chances of building trust. Victims can't trust villains, by definition. When we picture ourselves as victims, we excuse ourselves from taking action since we can't afford to be vulnerable.

We invite powerlessness when our internal self-talk sounds like: "It's not my fault," "It's all their fault," or "There's nothing I can do." These can be tempting to say to ourselves. Fortunately, the popular Serenity Prayer can be used to counter this mindset: "God, grant me the serenity to accept the things I cannot change, courage to change the things I can, and the wisdom to know the difference."

Today, I will take charge of my self-talk, starting with the rejection of victim and villain labels. Some things are my responsibility, and some things are not. Since I want my relationships to improve, I will find a way to move things forward. Motion begets more motion.

DAY 15: GOING DIRECT

Complaining to the wrong person damages trust, for several reasons:

- It takes a private matter public, needlessly amplifying its visibility, attention, and stress.
- It doesn't solve the actual problem.
- It demonstrates to the person we're complaining to that we talk behind others' backs. "Hmm, I wonder what he's been saying about me?"
- It causes factions to build within the organization (us vs. them).

Loyalty to the absent is a useful concept in our trust-builder's toolbox. This means refusing to talk negatively about Jerome when Jerome is not nearby. By acting in this way, we earn a reputation for being respectful and trustworthy, and we avoid feeling guilty when we run into Jerome!

So, while it can be more uncomfortable, we want to take matters up with the source. Indirect routes sow dissent, erode credibility, waste valuable time, and solve little. Sure, it can be helpful to enlist someone as a confidential sounding board. We just need to watch out for the slippery slope that leads to dishonorable talk and gossip.

Meetings after the official meetings are often where this disloyalty surfaces. At crunch time, we go along with authority or the popular opinion to avoid making a scene, or so we think. Then, after the meeting, we feel at liberty to share our honest opinions or criticisms with a select few. It's at this moment that trust-builders reveal our true colors. We may not have felt comfortable sharing our full opinion with the group; this has happened to every-body. But now that we clearly know what it is, we go find a private moment with the right person—usu-ally the decision-maker—instead of chattering in the hallway and eroding trust.

On this day, I will go to the source of the issue or conflict. I know that addressing concerns in a pri-vate way builds trust even amid short-term discom-fort. When it's my turn, I hope that others will return this courtesy!

DAY 16: HEAD GAMES

We want to avoid the trap of using manipulation to get our needs met. Sooner or later it will backfire and erode the trust that we have already built.

Head games come in a variety of flavors, yet they share a common element: a belief that the end justifies the means. Withholding pertinent information, taking shortcuts, pretending that things are different from reality, outright lying, and similar methods reveal a fundamental unwillingness to trust others to handle the truth.

Another reason we resort to manipulation: we sometimes feel personally responsible for the behavior of other people. We then try to handle them "just so" to get them to act a certain way (See Day 51, *Responsible for vs. to*).

Here's a common (and mistrusting) thought: "I'm not sure she can deal with this information, so it's probably best if I keep it quiet *for her own good*."

This is the permission slip we give ourselves for manipulating others. Shielding others from the whole truth is the exact opposite of trusting behavior.

A far more constructive approach is to level with them, encourage them, and coach them with all the facts at our disposal.

Today, I remember how it felt to be manipulated, and so I refuse to do this to others. I share the truth, the whole truth, and nothing but the truth—and trust the other person to react wisely, as a responsible adult. They deserve the facts.

DAY 17: VALUE OTHERS

We know what it feels like to be undervalued: small, unappreciated, and sometimes even resentful. Naturally, trust can be elusive at these times; we're unlikely to take risks when we're feeling this way. Many attitudes and behaviors can belittle a person, so as trust-builders we must learn to remain watchful.

For example, do we stop everything else and give others our complete attention? Do we encourage folks to share opinions that differ from ours? Do we focus on their unique talents instead of the skills they lack? Do we ask them questions? And listen fully to their answers? Without correction?

We search for ways to convey the *feeling* of being valued; it's not a specific formula. Let's look at an example: for most people under 25, answering a just-arrived text message during a conversation is common and ordinary, whereas doing it while speaking with someone over 50 can cause that person to feel disrespected. In time this distinction will fade, yet the concept holds.

Okay, but which is the correct etiquette? No hard rule applies here. Valuing someone always comes down to the individual.

With every interaction, we want to preserve others' dignity and right to their own individual worldview, regardless of how we may feel about it. We want to value them as unique, gifted people. Out of respect for the relationship, we should be patient and allow trust to grow over time.

On this day, I will make sure that those I interact with feel they matter to me as people, beyond the task or discussion at hand.

DAY 18: SAFE HARBOR

Trust is won or lost when emotions run high. Others are drawn to us if we earn a reputation for keeping a cool head in a storm. Independent of their role in an organization, trustworthy people emerge during a crisis. In a crunch, people seek out those who appear calm and in control.

How we respond in pressure situations can make a dramatic difference in the amount of safety those around us feel and, therefore, in the trust we earn. They may eventually forget the predicament itself, but they'll likely remember how they felt when we were nearby.

Emotional, highly charged, or panicked reactions are understandable, but they don't engender confidence. It takes rational thinking to identify available options, sort through them, and select the best course of action.

And even when the best response is unclear, a calming influence can still be helpful. This can certainly be taken too far: we can't afford to become detached or aloof lest others discount us as uncaring people. Neither highly emotional nor robotic responses offer much comfort. A reassuring smile goes a long way.

Most of us know the story: Captain Chesley "Sully" Sullenberger, on January 15, 2009, after losing both engines in a bird strike, landed his plane in the Hudson River, saving all 155 passengers and crew. His calmness under pressure was legendary. Like Sully, many first responders, emergency room personnel, dads, moms, teachers, bosses, and just about anyone can find themselves in overwhelming situations. Those who can breathe through it, remain composed, and bring some order to the chaos will win others' trust and confidence (and maybe even a movie contract).

Today, I will soothe another person as I remain calm, regardless of the situation. My undisturbed response builds trust by encouraging others to approach me when the going gets tough in the future.

DAY 19: FOLLOW ME

Who needs trust? I'm in charge!

We've all seen her: the manager who's been awarded that prime leadership position, and who, now that she's in charge, promptly forgets what it was like to work for a bully.

From experience, we know that if we don't trust our leaders, the most they usually get is our *compliance*. If the company is lucky, our parents or former leaders instilled in us a good work ethic that prevents us from full abdication. Inwardly we suspect that clueless bosses don't care much about us as people and so we return the sentiment with the amount of effort we bring.

The converse is just as powerful. When trust exists, there is no limit to the amount of profound, personal influence a leader can have. Trust overcomes mistakes, weak strategy, and bad execution. It also makes these problems less likely to occur. Why?

Because the work team becomes a stronger unit and its members won't, through inaction, allow it to fail.

Those who lead without first building trust in their relationships don't have the impact they think they do. The good news is that building trust is not complicated. It's often challenging, yes, but superior intellect is not necessary.

What if we work for a boss who doesn't seem to care about trust? Can we still be effective trust-builders? The answer is a resounding "yes." Our behaviors and trustworthiness are what this workout is all about. I would add a reminder that we have a responsibility to be loyal to the absent (See Day 15, *Going Direct*), and that includes our boss.

Today, I will look beyond my role and rank to connect with those I wish to influence. I will keep my ego in check and remember that gaining people's compliance is not enough. I want to deserve their trust.

DAY 20: I DON'T KNOW. CAN YOU HELP ME?

These are some of the hardest words to say, even though acknowledging we need help can be liberating and useful. Admitting our uncertainty can do much to catalyze our relationships and build trust, too.

The older we get, the more others rely on us and the less apt we are to admit our need for growth. We don't want to feel vulnerable. It's distasteful to confess that what we're doing, no matter how well-intentioned, just isn't working.

Plus, many of us get paid for what we know. We're just "supposed to know" certain things that come with the job, the territory, or the title—or so we tell ourselves. We buy into the lie that says we must prove ourselves worthy of that paycheck instead of the truth that no one knows all there is to know.

Human beings can take a lot of inconvenience, pain, and hardship. We are amazingly resilient. If coping with adverse conditions earned us medals, most of us would be Olympians. In the mental health and addiction world, there is a good reason that the final stage of fatigue and surrender is known as "hitting bottom." But in life, we don't earn points for the struggle, just for our results.

By asking for assistance, we let our guard down and become more approachable, which then opens up opportunities for mutual reliance and trust. It also sets a visible example for others so that maybe they'll call on us down the road.

Just for today, I can admit that something I'm wrestling with is bigger than me and that I need support. I concede my pain-endurance medal to others by asking for help. Today, I'll allow myself to be vulnerable and to count on someone else.

DAY 21: MOVING ON

Not all pain is the same. New pain is temporary trouble or discomfort associated with trying new things, solving fresh problems, or reaching new heights. Old pain comes from re-hashing intractable issues repeatedly, revisiting stubborn problems, or tolerating poor situations. I've observed that suffering accompanies old pain, not the new.

This concept directly relates to trust and the health of our relationships. If we solely focus on the disturbing aspects of today and yesterday, it becomes difficult for others to invest their trust in us. We're just no fun. If, on the other hand, we devote the significant part of our attention to moving into a new world, others are drawn to us and our energy.

In a meeting, would we rather discuss the incomplete action items or attack a new and exciting challenge? In sales, would we prefer to accept abuse from a nit-picking client or replace them with a customer who fits us better? As parents, would we sooner nag, chase, and punish the kids or spend quality time with them?

Just to be clear, I don't suggest that stubborn problems be abandoned. I'm saying that suffering and old pain are found together, and it's likely that a fresh approach will renew our enthusiasm and entice others into a positive outlook, trusting us to help create a better future.

None of us are immune to the problem of old pain. Some battles are hard-fought while others are just unwinnable. The pain of stretching and growing in new directions can bring a welcome joy to ourselves and others.

Today I'm going to have discomfort so it might as well be caused by new pain rather than old pain. I will shake off the need to completely resolve the past before moving forward in some way. Others trust me more when I'm going someplace positive.

DAY 22: TRUST DOOR

I n the world of trust-building, one of the patterns that can work against us is an unconscious habit of writing people off. It's a subtle thing, hardly noticeable as we go about our lives. Let's examine this pattern and see if it applies to us.

Over the years, hundreds of Building Trust clients have confided in me that they basically don't trust people. Something (or someone) happened along the way, usually early in their lives, which taught a harsh lesson: it was just safer not to trust. "I've always been like this. And if I'm honest, I'm okay with it."

Each of us has a Trust Door: a door to our vulnerable selves that only we control. I like to think of this door as having a sign above it that reads either "Welcome" or "Keep Back." We know what's written above our own door, but other people's signs are invisible.

Do we usually keep our Trust Door open or closed? Do people around us need to prove they're trustworthy before we open our door to them? Or are they allowed to walk freely through our door until they prove otherwise? Both of these styles are valid and carry their own risk. Knowing our own tendency is the critical thing here. But it's clear that trust can't be earned or given through a closed door.

Walls of isolation are usually built one brick at a time. Each time we write someone off, our wall gets a little bit higher. The price of this additional immediate security is often self-imposed quarantine. Beware of the tipping point when it becomes easier to lay brick than to expose ourselves to further risk. If our walls grow too high, we'll be the ones who get written off and the chances for connection will fade.

Today, I will open my Trust Door to one new person. I'll consciously give them a chance to earn my trust while I attempt to gain theirs. I don't want to live in quarantine. I want to live free and connected.

DAY 23: IN THE MOOD

Sometimes we need to take stock of our power to earn and extend trust. Why? Because this capacity changes over time, sometimes by a lot. We become readier to build trust by raising our self-awareness.

The factors listed below create a moving tapestry of influencers that have a big impact on us, especially if we're not paying attention. Taken together, they can compel us to advance trust, withhold trust, or operate somewhere in between.

TRUST FACTORS
- My age and stage of life
- The amount of risk I'm willing to live with
- The stability of my environment, past and present
- How much or little my "tribe" trusts others (never trust *those people*)
- My physical, mental, and emotional health

- My level of financial independence
- My faith and spiritual confidence
- Traumatic events (natural or man-made) that I've experienced
- Neglect or abuse I may have endured
- The rigidity of my thinking
- My sense of self and self-determination
- My work history (coworkers, bosses, organizations)
- The dependability of my family members, as a child or currently
- Whether I can and do express my thoughts openly and clearly

The effect of any individual factor can vary widely with each person; in combination, we see why the full spectrum of trust-ability is vast. If we're having trouble overcoming a trust issue with someone, maybe it's not the right time for us. No individual can possibly offset another person's full complexity.

Today I will pause, take stock, and check in with myself. If I can't build trust today, I'll gladly settle for moving one of my Trust Factors in a positive direction.

DAY 24: BEING RIGHT

How do I trust someone I know is dead wrong? We've discussed it a dozen times, and we just don't see eye-to-eye on _____ (fill in the blank). She can't convince me, and I can't seem to persuade her either.

People often tie agreement together with trust, but this is unnecessary and sometimes even unhelpful. We can enjoy trust without agreeing on things. We need honesty, caring, and reliability. In fact, open and kind disagreement between two people can lead to breakthroughs we would get in no other way.

I remember receiving a powerful email a few days after one of my Building Trust Experience workshops. After eleven years without contact, this client reunited with his father "... because I chose to allow my dad to be wrong."

Back in driver's education, they gave us a great example of this. Four vehicles arrive simultaneously at a four-way stop. If each driver then feels justified to speed across the intersection (after all, each was there *first*), they will end up dead. They will be "dead right."

Everyone is entitled to their own perspective. One of the fastest ways to destroy trust is to try to force our views onto someone else. We can try to inform, persuade, or convince others to come around to our way of thinking, but ultimately the choice is theirs. If we truly value the person and the relationship, we will respect them enough to honor their right to disagree. It's even possible that we're the ones who might need to change!

Today, I refuse to end up dead right. I will look for an opportunity to connect with someone who disagrees with me. I can learn to see past the discord and build a bridge to the person.

DAY 25: POLITE-ING ALL OVER EACH OTHER

When we act overly nice and sweet to one another but refrain from sharing matters of substance, I call it *polite-ing all over each other*, and as far as trust is concerned, it's a bad sign.

Don't get me wrong; civility and courtesy are important to any good relationship. How we treat a person helps to convey how much we value them. But if all we do is exchange pleasantries, any trust that does exist is shallow indeed.

During team formation, most people automatically drop into the polite mode. While getting acquainted, individual members scan the environment. We socialize with those who look and act as we do, hidden agendas stay hidden, risk is avoided, and personal disclosure is rare. We evade conflict with our smiles. This is normal and to be expected. But if we've spent much time with another person and the relationship continues to hover in over-polite sweetness, it's likely that a trust barrier of some kind exists.

Also, if a relationship hits a rough patch and falls back into polite-ing all over each other for very long, trust remains low. An icky conversation is probably necessary—and the sooner the better (See Day 49, *The Icky Place*).

Another area of over-politeness to watch for: emails. If our choice of language has to be so perfect that we risk upsetting someone, we will likely fail anyway. Why? Because we recognize a well-packaged email when we see one. They tick. Emails among trusted parties dispense with ceremony, contain typos, just say it, and reflect easy rapport.

Since some cultures prize politeness more than others, we must temper this idea to the specific situation.

Today, I will pay attention to interactions that are laden with over-politeness, mine or another's. It's a clue I may need to move that relationship to a better place.

DAY 26: WHOOPS! NOW WHAT?

We're having a productive, friendly conversation with another person when wham, it blows up on us. We know this because the other party becomes visibly aggressive or closed down. The next few seconds determine whether a trust deposit or a withdrawal is made.

We've all unknowingly said or done the wrong thing. We touch on a sore subject, trigger someone's insecurity, or treat an important topic insensitively and the other person's expression changes in a nanosecond.

When trust is low, guardedness or misinterpretation of intent can cause rapid derailments. When trust is high, derailments can also occur—defenses are down and excitement leads to carelessness. Regardless of how we triggered this bear trap, we want to extricate ourselves before we cause more damage. Alas, a common mistake is made right here: *we keep pushing.*

What happens when we keep talking to (or at) an aggressive person? Naturally, they get louder and more upset. Emotions take over, debate or argument ensues, and we compete with each other. Trust goes out the window.

What happens when we keep talking to (or at) a person who has shut down on us? They close off even more, bail out altogether, or leave. This is usually when we hear surrender words: "whatever," "fine," "you're the boss," or even "yes, honey."

I only know one way to rescue oneself from this situation: stop pushing, apologize, and give them the floor. Admit we are off-track, offer them a moment to breathe, and then ask a gentle, probing question. This returns us to a two-way discussion as nothing else can. If we run away or accept their surrender, we give up on trust.

Today, I won't make an unproductive situation worse by continuing to talk. To build trust, I'll invite the other person to join me in calm discourse.

DAY 27: THE PRICE TAG

n my Building Trust Experience workshops, I ask clients to identify the consequences of mistrust and unresolved conflict. They have no trouble coming up with a list. Answers vary, but common ones are:

- Added stress
- Disharmony
- Absenteeism
- Wasted time
- Depression
- Reduced productivity
- Poor decisions
- Isolation
- Apathy (giving up)
- Poor customer service/lost customers
- Declining health (headache, backache, strain, weakness)
- Unnecessary and costly employee turnover
- Eventually, lawsuits

Wow. When we step back to look at the price we pay for allowing mistrust to penetrate our lives, we can't help but wonder why. Despite the unfavorable outcomes, we abhor facing conflicts or we make believe they aren't happening.

It's comforting to know we aren't alone. These costs are familiar because we've all paid them at one time or another. Trust-builders stop pretending and learn to strike these costs from their budgets.

I acknowledge the cost of ongoing mistrust and unresolved conflict that surrounds me. Sometimes, awareness alone is a breakthrough. Whatever step I can take today to counter these forces is worth my effort, even if the outcome may not be visible overnight.

DAY 28: OKAY-NESS

We're having a private conversation, just us and one other person. The setting is quiet, neutral, and relaxed. The exchange is going well—both are sharing thoughts and feelings in an unhurried way. We're listening to one another without competing over who's right. We're feeling safe and mutually valued.

Trust is growing, we can feel it, right here in the moment. Maybe we're revealing some personal views that few others would appreciate. We may even surprise ourselves with how open and vulnerable we are right now. It's a great feeling.

At this instant, someone else walks up to us and *everything changes*. How come? What happened?

Our human nature automatically kicks in; we go into protection mode. That moment of shared authenticity vaporizes. We shield ourselves, our partner, and the newcomer as well. On a dime, we switch from vulnerable dialog to managing what I call "okay-ness." We avoid embarrassment by moving to harmless, innocuous topics—even mid-sentence if we have to. We ensure that the three of us are *okay*.

This is why I strongly recommend that trust-building conversations—those dealing with sensitive or icky subjects—be conducted in a private place that is void of interruptions. When it comes to trust, often the only way through it in a safe, authentic way is one-to-one.

Management-by-walking-around is a popular technique to improve a leader's visibility and learn what's happening in the organization. It's effective, but chatting beside a workstation or office is prone to being overheard and interrupted, so okay-ness rules. Risk-free, friendly banter is not enough to build strong employee trust.

I know that a safe, private, undisturbed setting is the best way to handle sensitive conversations. As I deal with intense subjects today, I'll insist on it!

DAY 29: THANK YOU

Dig through class photos from the first or second grade or from a kid's activity in which we participated. What's the very first thing we do? That's right, we rapidly scan past all the other little ones in a blur until we spot our own sweet (or dorky) face. We pause and drink in our younger self. Don't feel bad; everybody does this. The question is, why?

I submit that it's simple and basic: we, ourselves, are privately our own favorite subject. We find our own face first because only then does the rest of the group seem interesting. Again, there is nothing amiss about this.

What does this silly and seemingly universal tendency have to do with building trust? A lot. We humans go about our lives thinking about ourselves more often than we'd care to admit. Our needs, our priorities, our job prospects, our feelings.

This is why a sincere thank you is so treasured. It shows others how valuable they are to you. And regardless of their outward reaction (some people automatically deflect appreciation), the thanked person feels warm inside. An authentic thank you is a significant trust deposit that costs only our time and attention.

Most of us were taught as children to say please and thank you as basic etiquette, along with chewing with our mouths closed and other courtesies. It's common for us to offer the perfunctory thank you in social situations. But a stop-in-your-tracks, heartfelt sign of gratitude is entirely different.

The converse is also true. When we act on other people's behalf, we do so *in opposition* to our default self-centeredness, which is often why we feel we deserve to be thanked. An owed thank you that goes unfulfilled is likely perceived as a trust withdrawal. (Sorry, I didn't make the rules.)

Today, I will recognize and thank those who go out of their way for me. It's a gift that builds goodwill and trust.

DAY 30: LETTING GO

These days it seems the moment we resolve a problem, something comes along that forces us to reexamine our solution. Change is endless and sometimes overwhelming.

Change also carries the threat of loss. When asked to change, we must replace the familiar and comfortable with the unfamiliar. At best this is unsettling; at worst, terrifying. We want so hard to hold onto our current trapeze that we aren't willing to let go so we can miss grabbing the one(s) that may carry us forward.

Yet change also brings opportunity. A quick review of the changes we've already overcome demonstrates we're capable of major adjustments when needed. When facing a present fear, we often forget our own resiliency.

Returning to the trapeze illustration, picture a male "catcher" hanging upside down at the knees on one trapeze, arms outstretched and ready. Now picture a woman holding onto another trapeze by the hands and swinging toward the man. What is the catcher's job here? *To catch her in mid-air.* What is the woman's job? *To let go and be caught.* It is not to "help" the man—the last thing they need is for both sets of hands to be flailing around. No. Her job is to trust that he will be there and make the catch.

On day one for this maneuver, both gymnasts wore harnesses, the safety net was up close, and vocal communication was constant. We know that trust like this requires a long time, the gradual introduction of additional risk, and a lot of repeated practice. Confidence replaces fear—one (successful) catch at a time.

Just like every other trust-building endeavor.

I know that by building trust, I offer confidence in times of change and difficulty. People willingly let go of their current situation only when they trust they can make it through safely. Today, let me be an encouragement to my fellow travelers.

DAY 31: LAZY BRAIN

"Jane, please come to Bruce's office. Jane to Bruce's office, please." What's Jane's immediate internal reaction? "Uh-oh." It's often true even if Jane and Bruce have a great relationship. The sympathetic looks she gets on her way to his office don't help much either.

We resolve to buy a particular model vehicle. Suddenly, we begin to see many more of these on the road. Wow, we think, we must be justified in our selection since so many other (clearly smart) people have done likewise.

Pick someone who differs from ourselves along the lines of politics, race, religion, gender, or age. On some level, we can already somewhat predict their thoughts and beliefs. Okay, now switch positions. How accurate is their perception of what we think and believe?

These examples illustrate how our brains vigilantly look for patterns. We are amazingly efficient at scanning our environment and drawing conclusions from minimal data. If we've had experience with a situation, a group of people, or a feeling, this sensitivity internalizes; it becomes nearly automatic. The brain stores these recognized patterns to save the energy of reevaluating what we repeatedly observe, again, for efficiency. It's why the details of our commute to work fade once it becomes routine. The brain stores the familiar so it can free itself to focus attention on the unknown or more significant.

But there's another way to see this dynamic—I call it *lazy brain*. The brain wants to stop working so hard. And herein lies another trust-preventing trap door. Not all bosses are scary. Just because cars are on the road doesn't mean their owners are happy. Stereotypes shut down our willingness to listen and extend trust.

Just because something feels familiar does not mean it fits the pattern in my mind. Today, I will treat every person and situation as a fresh opportunity. My relationships deserve my active brainpower!

DAY 32: CHECKERS OR CHESS?

I f only we could treat everyone the same way, like the game pieces in checkers.

Marcus Buckingham*, the author of several books on employing our strengths, says that great team members resemble the uniqueness and complexity of the pieces on a chessboard more than they do the "sameness" in a game of checkers. Buckingham says that creative leaders maximize performance by figuring out and utilizing the unique strengths, talents, and motivations of each individual team member. By contrast, uninspired leaders assume that every member pretty much responds the same way to all issues, techniques, and challenges.

In building trust, we learn to adapt our engagement style to each specific person. This doesn't make us false or manipulative unless we take it too far. Instead, it shows we value the unique combination of qualities each person represents. In short, we don't treat bishops and knights the same way; we maximize their strengths and limit the risk from their weaknesses.

I can't leave this subject without a word on "well-rounded" professionals; I'm not a big fan. I like working with people who keep their distinctiveness, or in other words, their "edges." Well-rounded people believe the societal propaganda that they need to become checker pieces to get along in life. Wouldn't you prefer to be treated like the unique, remarkable person you really are?

Today, I will look for the uniqueness in the people I meet. By valuing them for it, I have a healthier chance of building trust between us. I know better than to assume that everyone is the same.

Bonus: If I see a well-rounded person today, I'll encourage her to assert more of her distinctive, natural self!

*Marcus Buckingham, *First Break All the Rules*, published by Gallup Press

DAY 33: EXPECT HUMANITY

When we get past the idea that we *deserve* certain treatment from others, we set reasonable expectations. Once this happens, we discover that other people aren't much different than we are: flawed human beings who mess things up from time to time. And it's much easier to extend our trust to a real person than to a superhero, or scoundrel, who doesn't live up to our expectations. It takes longer, yes, but when their inevitable blunder materializes, the trust we've built together doesn't shatter.

Our society puts great value in high expectations, and rightly so. When we purchase a product or service, we expect it to work as advertised—without fail, and for a long time. Over time we become loyal to particular brands, whether they be clothing, cleaning products, or cars. The trouble arises when we expect the same flawless performance from individuals that we do from automated equipment, processes, and quality systems. Before a typical product hits the shelves, it's been inspected, tested, and certified. Well, people aren't products; we're only human, after all.

When my expectations of a person grow unrealistic, I often remind myself that *we live on planet Earth, not planet Fair.* It doesn't matter much what I think I deserve from this person. I'm not entitled to something beyond their ability to supply it.

I've had the privilege to serve on multiple mission trips to the poor in Guatemala. Among the many blessings that the locals showed me was a profound joy amid their need. Community spirit was contagious; the trust among villagers was palpable and intense. They depended on each other for their assets and contributions. The things they lacked were not the focus. In the absence of entitlement and perceived unfairness, I was moved by their effortless cohesion.

Today, I'll let go of my sense of entitlement. I'll stay firmly planted on planet Earth, lower my expectations, and celebrate the assets of the people around me. This only seems, well, fair.

DAY 34: BETTER BEATS PERFECT

Momentum. It's what we're looking for in business and relationships. Get started, grow slowly, accelerate, and eventually arrive at a point where the parties thrive.

How often do we sabotage long-term success by rushing things to happen before their natural time? How many ideas stall in the pursuit of flawlessness instead of launching in an awkward or clumsy first attempt? Continuous improvement usually beats delayed perfection; we begin to harvest the rewards of early progress.

Momentum can be felt. The instant we get something started, our minds freshly engage and look for ways to make it faster, easier, and more enjoyable. Ask a newlywed or cell phone designer.

For some reason, we haven't executed lots of our good ideas. When we insist on the perfect implementation plan, we often don't get started. This hamstrings us with business, life, and other people. Frequently, in other words, the only thing holding us back is us.

When it comes to trusting someone, occasionally we get caught in all-or-nothing thinking as well. We fret over conjuring a precise plan to transform the bond into a trusting one, or we hold out—hoping for a miracle. Such thinking is the enemy of momentum. We need only remind ourselves to get started, to keep the lines of communication open, and to believe that better beats perfection. Once we get (re) engaged, our minds will continue moving us along a positive trajectory.

Today, I give myself permission to try something without needing to get it exactly right on the first attempt. If I can get myself into motion, I am on my way.

DAY 35: CRYSTAL CLEAR

The topic of relationship boundaries is an important and complex one. I'm no expert on this—in fact, I've struggled most of my life with establishing and maintaining consistent boundaries. However, the healthiest people I know do a great job in this area; I admire them.

These people make conscious determinations about three things when it comes to relationships: what they prefer, what they will tolerate, and what they find unacceptable. They actively encourage what they like, endure without grudge what they'll accept, and vigorously defend what they consider the boundaries of unacceptable behavior. In doing this, they're able to preserve and strengthen their sense of self and well-being.

I admire the clarity of my interactions with these people, even when I disagree with them, because they tend to respect others as much as they do themselves. They know who they are. They're solid,

consistent, and predictable. I know who I'm dealing with and this is the foundation for trust. People
without clear and consistent boundaries are harder
to trust because they're less reliable.

Children test limits; it's what they do. We learn
that if we say this word, Dad smiles encouragingly,
that word earns a stern look, and the bad word lands
us in time-out (or in my day, the bar of soap). Later,
when Mom uses the time-out words, we get confused
and have trouble trusting. What gives here? Why
does Mom get away with this? Which rule applies?

Clear and consistent boundaries build trust.

*Today I will examine and shore up my boundaries
so I can be more consistent and trustworthy in the
days to come.*

DAY 36: FOOLS AND ENEMIES

For valid reasons, we lament the loss of tolerance and respect in our society. Elected officials take polarizing stances and use language that demonize those who disagree with them. Users of social media hide behind relative anonymity to post hurtful rants or one-sided worldviews. Civility in public discourse and diplomatic negotiation itself feels endangered. If our "side" is not in power, we may live in anger and fear—as if the other side were a sworn enemy.

Regardless of whether we choose to participate in this maelstrom of opposition, it's all around us. So, gut check time: how well do we shut off this way of thinking when we interact with our friends, coworkers, church community, or even our family? We may hide it (even from ourselves), but the pattern of right/wrong, win/lose, and friend/foe reasoning is not so easy to shake.

If our goal is building trust with real human be-ings, we need to let go of these polarizing tenden-cies. We must find room in our minds and hearts for those who see the world differently than we do. Bonds, and therefore trust, can't develop unless there is space in the relationship for disagreement without it being interpreted as disrespect or foolish-ness. Nobody trusts fools or enemies.

In my own life, I've discovered that changing my self-talk is the most effective way to break out of this oppositional bias and open the road to trust. By saying these things to myself, I can slow down my blood flow, remind myself of the other's humanity, and build unity instead of division:

- They're entitled to how they see the world.
- I can learn from an alternative viewpoint.
- Assume them reasonable/rational: why might they think or behave this way?
- It's not about me; what's the bigger issue?
- Find the common ground with this person!

All sorts of trustworthy people happen to disagree with us on important matters.

Today I will look past my disagreements and find ways to overcome any tendencies I have to label oth-ers as enemies or fools. Diplomacy can start with me.

DAY 37: RESULTS MATTER

For today, let's look at winning itself. Let's suspend whether the winners win with honor and respect toward others (which, for the record, I highly espouse). Case in point: in 2016, millions of Americans voted a perceived "winner" into the presidency despite having a controversial record. Regardless of one's politics, it's hard to escape the conclusion that winners draw others to themselves.

I don't suggest that this is fair, or just, or how things should be. I'm merely going to an icky place in the trust-builder's reality: habitual winners have more impact and influence than routine losers. Look around your own life. I think you'll agree.

No matter the arena, winning is compelling whether it's in science, politics, sports, battle, business, career, or even parenting (check social media). Readers of this book want to build more trust, so it's worth our while to examine what it takes to improve our winning percentage.

Winners ask for help, especially for new knowledge and support. They work on their own game first, expending little time focusing on others. Rarely satisfied, achievers bounce back quickly when they lose. They want the ball and the opportunity, and then come through when it matters. "Put me in, coach!"

Winners avoid excuses, understanding that obstacles are given and are meant to be overcome. They hate losing—this may seem obvious, but many fine people are comfortable with just "playing." Winners always keep score and understand that daily habits (the fundamentals) are the real secret to success.

Many people have great relationships yet still struggle to earn others' faith and trust. If this is you, maybe it's time to up your winning percentage.

Today I will take a good look at the fire in my belly for winning. Have I become complacent or accepted mediocrity? If I want others to trust me more, I may need to add some fuel to the fire!

DAY 38: YOU, WE, AND I

You're a liar. We are having a hard time trusting you. *I felt stupid when I found out what you said was untrue.*

You keep dominating the conversation. Others would like to get a word in here too, you know. *I have something to say.*

Your drinking is a problem. A lot of us are frustrated and worried about you. *I love you, and it pains me to see you like this.*

We've been encouraged to use I-statements before. Like other trust-building concepts in this book, getting the hang of it takes time and practice. I've included the three examples above to illustrate how and why developing this habit is worth our attention.

A genuine I-statement speaks in terms of ourselves and our own feelings. It takes 100 percent personal ownership for the message being delivered, it's clear, and it seeks no harm. So "I feel that you stink," doesn't count.

The beauty of I-statements is that they can be personal, non-preachy, direct, and non-negotiable. They don't accuse, label, or raise the hackles of the other person. They build trust because they often reveal something important in the relationship, which can then be dealt with more constructively.

Now let's look again at the We-statements above. This is what can happen when well-meaning people don't fully invest. They land somewhere between an accusatory You-statement and a truly powerful I-statement. Unfortunately, the message often gets softened, and the lack of personal ownership makes it much less effective. Purposeful trust-builders avoid both You- and We-statements.

Today I will build trust by owning my thoughts and feelings 100 percent. I'll express them to others without blame, accusation, or expectation.

DAY 39: FIRST COMES TRUST, THEN COMES PEACE

lessed are the peacemakers, for they shall be called sons of God. Matt 5:9 ESV

Regardless of one's upbringing, most of us learn early that keeping the peace is highly valued by the adults around us, and for good reason. To get along with others, kids must learn self-control at home, in the classroom, and on the playground. Unfortunately, many of us received this lesson in the extreme, excelling at peacekeeping while our inner thoughts, feelings, or needs were discounted or even buried. Our young selves, reinforced by our loved ones, equated quiet with peace.

And yet the absence of vocal argument is not peace. Far from it, as anyone will tell you who's been required to hug a younger sibling (when they'd enjoy punching them much more). That was a forced cease-fire. Peace comes at night, in the shared bedroom, when the kids privately talked through the conflict and forgave each other, falling asleep know-ing they had each other's back. Sounds like a bless-ing to me.

Real peace arrives when trust is built or restored.

What "peacekeeping" techniques do we employ today? Do we dodge embarrassment by letting peo-ple off the hook? Do we use humor to distract or cut the tension instead of easing into the uncomfortable-ness? Do we swallow our own thoughts and feelings like the old days? Do we find a safe topic to fight about but hide the core, vulnerable issue?

These behaviors are merely self-imposed cease-fires; the trust-eroding problem is still there, smoth-ering our chances for peace. We're watching our own back.

Today I will be an authentic maker of peace by not settling for a cease-fire. By employing my trust-build-ing skills, I will bless those around me with peace itself.

DAY 40: DOES THAT MAKE SENSE?

My pet peeves annoy me. Does that make sense? Certain unimportant things get under our skin, and only ours. Does that make sense? For me, one of these things is the question, "Does that make sense?" Arrgh!

It's an innocent question, but every time I encounter it, I can't help but hear, "Are you smart enough to follow me, Bruce?" I'm always tempted to respond with, "No. It makes no sense. Please try again." I automatically assume the person asking, "Does that make sense?" wants to convert my "yes" answer into an agreement with whatever they just said. I feel like I'm being forced along a cattle chute. Drives me crazy. Does that make sense?

Notice how silly and unproductive this habit can be. Here I am trying to demonstrate effective communications and trust-building skills only to get totally distracted from the conversation and fall through a trap door of my own making. If we let them, our pet peeves will do that to us endlessly. Overcoming this distraction by releasing our personal irritations can keep us engaged in the discussion, show interest, and build trust. Note: The simple practice of brief, daily meditation can help with our focus and self-awareness.

Even before babies learn to talk, they connect quite effectively. Parents discern the differences between the cries of their infant because hungry, pained, wet, tired, and scared all sound unique. Communication is not about language—it's more fundamental than that. It lies in the desire of the listener (parent) to focus on the communicator (baby) until its message is accurately received.

Intrusions that get in the way of focusing on others during communication must be fought. Our pet peeves are merely the obvious ones. Plus, nobody likes their language or behavior nitpicked. Does that make sense?

Today I will sharpen my listening skills by valuing the other person enough not to get distracted by my own pet peeves. They don't matter. The other person does!

DAY 41: TRUSTING AGAIN

The most common question I get is, "How does someone restore trust with me?" Typically it's about a person we can't easily cast out of our lives. After a little digging, the core question often turns out to be, "How can I ever trust a person again after what they did/didn't do or said/didn't say?"

It's common for people to look for ways that others can re-build trust with us (the innocent victim) instead of asking what we can contribute here. Yet without our active, intentional participation, the other person has no chance.

First, when we're ready, we must *choose* to open the door to trust. While we sit on the fence (or worse, opt to write people off), trust is at a standstill. Write down or say aloud: "As of right now, I am open and willing to see where this goes."

In due time, we may be ready to take the next step: *forgiveness*. By forgiving the person of their past behavior, we stop paying rent in our minds to the resentment that keeps us stuck. Forgiving is not forgetting; it is merely releasing both of us from the anchor of the past. Sometimes this is hard, spiritual work.

At some stage the release becomes real, not just an intention; we'll know when we get there. Then we can move on to step three: *talking with the person* about our desire to reestablish a stronger relationship. It's best to get this out on the table so that both parties can invest in the goal.

Our last step is *allowing them fresh opportunities to earn back our confidence.* It won't happen overnight, so patience is needed. But if the relationship matters enough, many past difficulties can be overcome. It helps to remember that the other person is only human. Be prepared for a long road.

To trust another person again, I accept that things may never be the same as they once were. Yet today I will do my part by opening the door, forgiving, being honest, or giving them room to succeed. The rest is up to them.

DAY 42: THE CULTURE VULTURE

Did you hear about so-and-so? That's not my job. Don't be a suck-up. In the real world, what is tolerated is endorsed. Today's workout focuses on the culture around us and our personal duty to help make it trustworthy and respectful.

When we tolerate unhealthy habits in our family, team, or workplace, our silence indicates implied approval. An off-color joke, the ridicule of someone who's not around to defend herself, or an outright lie—we witness these situations and are often unable or unwilling to oppose them. We can even get drawn into the "fun." I'm not talking about light-hearted, playful ribbing among friends. I mean the sharp-edged words that leave a bad taste or lasting harm. Culture vultures scan the ground, seeking someone to tear down or a tasty morsel to chew on.

Environments of disregard, deception, and dis-harmony are too familiar. No matter how good we may be at trust-building, a toxic culture can creep into our own psyches. To fit in, our standards erode over time.

Can one person change the culture of the family or team? Yes and no. Yes, one person can lead the way with their own behaviors and habits, but often they can't make a lasting cultural difference without help. The best way to gain cultural momentum is to identify and recruit more like-minded people to the cause.

At home or at work, it's our culture, too. Each of us agrees to participate in health or harm. It's true that some cultural issues are more extensive or pervasive than what one person can change. In these cases, sometimes it's enough to constructively shine a flashlight on the problem. We may discover, as many do, that we are far from alone in our dissatisfaction. The unwillingness to tolerate the intolerable may need to start with us.

Today I will privately address a toxic behavior I notice permeating our culture. Suspicion and mistrust are contagious, and I will do my part to make our team more trustworthy.

DAY 43: EXPANDING OUR TRIBE

Many of us believe that a central trust element is aligned thinking. Let's challenge this by examining the advantages of forming a broad network of people with whom we disagree.

Often, despite our first reactions, the wisest advice we get is from people who see the world quite differently from ourselves. They are much more likely to ask that unpleasant yet vital question. We still get to chart our course, but we do so from a broader perspective. Yes, this may include listening to *everyone* at family meals.

Developing patience and respect for the "other" is a core trust-building ability; the more we exercise this skill, the stronger it becomes. And as our circle widens, the more influence we have. Plus, by knowing more people, the highly trusted person relies less on her private thoughts and resources and can tap into the knowledge and good will of her network.

As we expand our tribe, opportunities to practice communicating our own vulnerable, half-baked thoughts emerge. Great joy is found in those relationships where it is safe to differ, and yet both parties can be themselves. We trust them enough to ask for help to challenge, fine-tune, and polish our ideas.

Consider the opposite. Who trusts those who limit themselves to an insular group of like-minded individuals? Those who are looking for zealous agreement with what they already believe. Because so little is actually confronted, it's harder to learn effective listening and communication skills.

A great trust-building goal: finding new trustworthy people who disagree with us!

Today I will actively respect someone who disagrees with me over an important matter. By fully understanding their point of view, I learn from them and widen my appreciation for how they see things. In so doing, my world grows.

DAY 44: IN YOUR FACE

We communicate with others in countless ways today. Text, phone calls, email, voicemail, letters, sticky notes, gestures across the hallway, instant messaging, video chat, plus every style of meeting. New methods are invented more rapidly than old ones disappear; our choices for how to get someone a message just keep growing.

Each method serves its purpose but comes with pros and cons. We don't have space for a complete analysis, but which method provides the best chance of building trust? When the subject is dicey or complicated, we need to get in their face (constructively, of course).

Studies show that the vast majority of information-transfer between people is nonverbal (posture, facial expressions, readable emotions, pace, volume, tone, and gestures). Consciously and otherwise, we convey a world of meaning and depth through our nonverbals. We lose much when we strip out all this flavor.

We already know that words are not enough. We add emojis to a text or email lest they are misinterpreted. We carefully construct our electronic communications and review them several times before hitting Send. Words can only do so much.

In general, when high trust exists between two people, other tools can be more safely used without causing a misunderstanding. They're safer, but not safe. It's common to deliver a poorly worded message and find out the hard way that trust has been damaged.

In-person face time is still the safest choice for building trust, especially for hard or potentially emotional topics. Live video chat is okay (if it's fast), or perhaps a phone call. Text, email, voicemail, and other one-way methods just don't cut it.

On important issues, today I will interact face-to-face. My relationships deserve it.

DAY 45: SHARE THE LOAD

We all have activities we enjoy and at which we excel. They don't feel like work to us, even though others may struggle with them. They bring us a strong sense of satisfaction, and we look forward to the next opportunity to tackle them. We *own* them.

These are the very tasks that produce a great deal of mutual trust when we can (gulp) pry our fingers away and teach someone else to take them over. Not only do we thereby give others the chance to earn our trust, but our investment in helping to grow another person is a meaningful deposit in the relationship. They know we are in their corner because they recognize the sacrifice we made by entrusting them with our "baby."

Perfectionists who prefer to do things themselves are probably sweating. I get it. Others won't do it your way. Until they learn, they will make mistakes and miss the fine points—while you become frustrated.

Take heart; you're on the right track. The trust lessons you will learn throughout this process of letting go are profound. I encourage you to keep going, even if you get bruised along the way.

There are two common mistakes to avoid. First, don't under-prepare the person by giving unclear guidance or expectations. Second, don't grow upset with them or the process by grabbing the task back or abdicating it altogether.

The job needs to be done correctly, within reason, so that our trust is well-founded. The importance of the task governs how much accountability and visibility needs to be built into this hand-over. Negotiate a plan for ongoing communication such that both parties can grow more comfortable over time. The frequency of check-ins will be primarily determined by how well things go. At some point, the transfer is complete and then we get to do this again!

Today I will choose something I love to do that another person can learn, too. By sharing the load, I will invest in them and build trust between us.

DAY 46: LOSING IT

I encourage authenticity and transparency, with good reason. Trust is built when others see the real people inside us. It's important to remember, however, that candor does not entitle us to lose control.

In getting our ideas across, we strive to be assertive. We may *inform* by sharing evidence or opinion. We may go further by trying to *convince* them of something. We may even attempt to *persuade* them to change their thinking. But let's say the person remains unconvinced or unwilling to budge. Here's the danger point. If we have more to tell and all our attempts at *assertiveness* have failed, we can slip into *aggressiveness* all too easily.

Heart rate up, adrenaline pumping, we keep pushing. Maybe we get sarcastic, raise our voice, become passive-aggressive, or even act out physically. We lose it. I remember shouting at my kids when they were little. Some part of me knew I had lost

control but at the moment I felt justified, and be-
sides, it seemed I couldn't help myself. The scared
looks on their faces brought me back to reality.

Since the foundation of trust is safety, any form
of aggression withdraws trust—at least temporarily.
The more power we have in the relationship (coach,
parent, boss, etc.), the more likely our behaviors are
seen as aggressive rather than assertive, so we have
to watch ourselves. A good clue is whether the other
person has shut down on us; if so, we've probably
crossed the line.

Occasionally, we'll find ourselves in this aggressive place; it happens to the best of us. We don't
want to end the encounter here, because we'd leave a
lasting impression that we're unsafe. Don't go down
with the ship and cause long-term damage. Instead,
take a deep breath, regain a sense of calmness, and,
if appropriate, apologize. Ask a question to get the
conversation back on track. Close only when both of
you feel safe and comfortable.

*Today I will remember that aggression and trust do
not co-exist.*

DAY 47: SELF-IMPOSED BUREAUCRACY

Aside from non-negotiable, externally imposed requirements such as laws, safety regulations, accounting standards, I refer today to our *self-imposed* rules.

There is a time and a place for rules, regulations, levels of authority, and the like. Healthy organizations need structure to function smoothly and predictably. Even families must sort out who does what and how often, so its members have a safe, clean, well-provisioned place to live.

Most of us rely on the rules so we can trust the world around us. When people step out of line, we know it and they do, too. This is all valid and useful. However, many rules actually *replace* trust, not build it. As a basic example, consider dress codes at work. Some HR manuals are lengthy and specific here, while others simply say, "Dress appropriately," and trust people to use good judgment.

It's generally true that where trust is high, fewer controls are necessary. Rules can get in the way of flexibility, change, negotiation, and relationship-building. They slow things down, add complexity, and create silos of accountability ("not my job" syndrome). The best rules are those that set up boundaries yet don't gunk up the works of interpersonal trust and collaboration. Don't write a new rule because you don't trust someone. Solve the real problem instead.

In my career, I've worked in various environments: startups, churches, medium-sized businesses, multinational corporations, and even the federal government. The bigger the organization, the more that bureaucracy seems to invade. Yet in every situation, I've experienced the thrill of working with great people who followed the external rules, while removing as many internal barriers as possible, leading to high levels of trust and lifelong friendships.

Today I seek to remove some bureaucracy in my life, where a rule keeps me from trusting others to act like adults. I know this will invite some risk back onto the shoulders of each of us—and then we can earn each other's trust going forward.

DAY 48: THE POPEYE MOMENT

When Popeye the Sailor, the 1920s cartoon hero, had run out of patience he used to say, "That's all I can stands. I can't stands no more!" Fortunately for Olive Oyl, his nearby can of spinach gave him the energy to turn things around. In life, few of us have such a handy solution.

On Day 22, *Trust Door*, we examined the risks and consequences of writing people out of our lives. Today we're doing the opposite: probing the costs of accommodating the ties that need to be severed.

To be clear: this book is about trust-building. We want that to happen, but success is surrounding oneself in meaningful, trusting, and growing relationships. It's not carrying the chronically unreliable as people to be rescued or projects to be fixed.

In 2000, Dr. Henry Cloud published *Necessary Endings: The Employees, Businesses, and Relationships That All of Us Have to Give Up in Order to*

Move Forward. He delved into the reasons we tend to hang on to people, jobs, and beliefs that no longer work for us or hold us back. One-sided, draining relationships. Dead-end jobs. Inherited biases against certain people groups.

Dr. Cloud compared our lives to a rosebush: untended, we carry along dead branches, sickly buds, and other distractions throughout our lives. Wise pruners trim things that prevent sunlight, water, and nutrients from nourishing the best blossoms.

Is our pain tolerance too high? Are we covering for others? Do we see "endings" as a personal failure? Sometimes, health requires tough but necessary trimming.

With open eyes, today I will review the people in my life who consistently withdraw my trust. Where I truly "can't stands no more," I give myself permission to move away from the person and wish them well. Those I do trust, including myself, will then get the best of my time and energy.

DAY 49: THE ICKY PLACE

The "icky place" is the pivotal spot in any one-to-one communication that reveals vital, often uncomfortable, emotion or information. Perhaps someone has moved below the surface to reveal a core issue. Or we've surprised ourselves by feeling secure enough to disclose more than we expected. Responses to this revelation can harm trust, yes, but unless we go there, rarely can trust be achieved.

Would life become nonstop intensity if this were the norm? By no means. As we level with each other, stress fades. The less we posture, the easier we solve our problems, find common ground, end toxic things quickly, and reach our goals.

But we don't *want* to go to the icky place. We pretend. We wear our best smile. We pray that time or God will solve the problem. Issues fester, relationships plateau, and stress accumulates. In time, it becomes hard to return to that relaxed, open, vulnerable condition that leads to breakthroughs and trust.

We settle for "getting along," "working together," or other versions of "good enough."

Honest exchanges tell the truth. *Open* ones share what's really going on. Spouses know this, as do parents of teenagers, or anyone who's watched politicians or managers cherry-pick through facts. The whole truth is what builds trust.

We must settle for ourselves how open we can afford to be. People will, by human nature, let each other down. Sound needs a medium like air or water to exist. Likewise, without risk, trust cannot occur. Only by revealing ourselves do we allow others to demonstrate their trustworthiness. Yes, or otherwise.

To build trust, step out on the limb and open yourself up. Pursue the nonverbal signal your partner has just given you. Ask the penetrating question. If that's too far, take a half-step. If it just doesn't feel safe, honor yourself; find another person you're more comfortable with, and try again.

Today, I'll build trust one relationship at a time, on the other side of the icky place.

DAY 50: THE MIRROR

How comfortable are we at holding our own gaze in the mirror?

Many of us who want more trust in our lives have a blind spot. I'll just say it: we don't trust ourselves much. And if we can't trust ourselves, we assume we can't trust others. Why would someone else have our best interests in mind when we, who *should* have it, can be so unreliable?

No other person knows us as well as we do. We see when we let ourselves down, make excuses, cheat on our own standards, rationalize our bad choices and behaviors, etc. As we do these things, we lose faith in ourselves. We then project this fundamental untrustworthiness onto others. Often, the strength of our trusting relationships correlates with how steady we can look ourselves in the eye.

Put another way, the greater the difference between who we present to the outside world and what we believe about ourselves on the inside, the more likely it is that we struggle with trust. When this gap is wide, extending trust to others feels scary—even foolish. Also, we can wonder if others' trust in us is well-placed since it's not based on who we really are—or so we fear.

Thankfully, as with the other concepts in this workout, progress can be made here, too. I've never met a person who would rate themselves as perfect on the self-trust scale; each of us is a work-in-progress. Over time, there are many things we can do to trust ourselves more, for example:

- Take better care of our spiritual, emotional, physical, and/or financial needs.
- Compare our inner thoughts to our outer realities. Make adjustments as needed and celebrate areas of alignment.
- Reexamine our standards. To build self-trust, they should be low enough to reach and high enough to matter.

Today I will look myself in the mirror and watch for opportunities to earn my own trust. The more I trust me, the further that trust can grow all around me.

DAY 51: RESPONSIBLE FOR VS. TO

At the grocery checkout, unnoticed, your four-year-old daughter pockets a candy bar. When you discover this in the parking lot, you are annoyed and embarrassed. Yes, she took it, but as the parent, you are responsible. So you return to the store to put it back or pay for it. This is the essence of being *responsible for* someone else: we are accountable for the outcomes of their decisions.

Fast-forward ten years. Your now fourteen-year-old daughter does the same thing. Big difference, right? With older kids, our job is to be *responsible to* them by teaching right from wrong and setting a good example. At this point in her life, she has begun to take *responsibility for* herself. She faces the consequences of her own choices. Life goes on, she reaches adulthood, and the transition completes.

Yet don't we sometimes forget this at work or other adult situations? Acting *responsible for* means we try to fix, protect, rescue, and control people. We carry their feelings and don't listen well. We feel anxious, fearful, and liable for what they might do. We get concerned with solutions, answers, circumstances, being right, and all the details. We expect them to live up to our expectations, so we occasionally end up manipulating them. It's exhausting!

In contrast, when we are *responsible to* others, we show encouragement and empathy. We listen fully and we level with them because they are carrying the ball, not us. We feel relaxed, free, and aware. We have high self-esteem regardless of what they do. We become a helper and a guide. We expect them to be responsible for themselves and their own actions, so we can trust and let go.

This change in mindset is profound. Energy is restored. We see the adults around us as fellow travelers, not projects. Accountability is more comfortable and better. Most battles of will tend to evaporate.

Today I will be responsible for only one adult: myself. If I carry the consequences of other people's choices, I won't learn to trust them. And they won't grow.

DAY 52: BY ASSOCIATION

Guilt by association is a well-known phenomenon. Often unfairly, people are assumed to be complicit in wrongdoing simply through the relationships they share.

Credibility by association works in a less obvious, although similar way. When we surround ourselves with trustworthy, dependable people, some of their credibility rubs off on us.

Years ago, my company promoted a "high standards" employee in the quality department to the role of supervisor. As a leader, his backbone, unfortunately, became a liability. He acted like a bully—subtly at first, but progressively bolder. In the months it took for senior management to sort out and rectify the problem, a lot of damage to our trusting environment was done. Out of fear, instead of bringing their quality questions to this supervisor, employees either concluded things on their own or worse: hid them. It was a painful episode for the company.

It took a long time to reestablish the credibility of our leadership team as a whole. Naturally, employees had assumed that management either endorsed this bullying behavior or was unable to stop it. The hard lesson: the credibility of one team member has a direct impact on the credibility of all—even those who believe they are powerless in the situation.

So it is with every group or team, regardless of the circumstances. And so it's incumbent upon the trust-builder to remain alert as to how their fellow crew members are perceived. If trustworthiness truly matters to us, we cannot afford to pretend that a teammate's behavior is irrelevant. We are not responsible for their choices, but since they are on our team, we have a responsibility to strengthen our collective reliability.

Today I will pay more attention to the credibility of my teammates. If there's a trustworthiness issue, I will constructively address it. Moreover, I'll remember that my own behavior reflects on my colleagues, for good or ill.

DAY 53: THE LONG ROAD BACK

Betrayal. The word alone can make us shiver, trigger our anger, or both. For someone to betray us, they must have already had our trust, which is why this wound is so deep and personal. We felt safe with them. Now, we don't.

Our anger at them may be justified, but the fear that we were fools to trust them in the first place can eat at us. In our frustration, we often stew over problems and think thoughts like, "What's wrong with me? Why didn't I see this coming? Am I gullible? Do others I trust right now really deserve it? How do I protect myself so it never happens again?"

The trouble, of course, is that nothing will reassure us that we can safely trust in the future. Only by risking again can this happen. And now that we've lost our innocence, it will likely be harder and take more time than it once did. After a betrayal, it's a long road back to trust because we must restore it with ourselves first, and then with others (See Day 41, *Trusting Again*).

The more intimate our damaged relationship (parent, spouse, sibling, boss, doctor, close friend), the deeper the injury and the longer the recovery period. And like other matters in the trust universe, there are levels of betrayal.

As a trust-builder, if you feel betrayed, I offer these suggestions:

- Get some spiritual help, in whatever form this means for you, to be patient.
- Avoid compounding the problem with your behavior. For example: publicly condemning your betrayer may paint you as untrustworthy yourself.
- Try to limit the reach of the betrayal to the specific person or circumstances.
- Try not to let others pay for the failings of one individual.
- You'll learn what you need to from the event as soon as you forgive yourself.

Today, I will limit the damage from any recent betrayals and continue to heal the wounds from old ones. I may need outside help to accomplish this, either from wise counselors or from spiritual sources.

DAY 54: CLIMBING THE LADDER

Before we can get somewhere else, we must know where we are. Trust-building is no different. Assessing my family, team, or business against certain rungs on a ladder can be helpful.

We start climbing on the ***Polite*** rung. This is where we play "nice," hide our thoughts, and avoid conflict. Well-meaning individuals want relationships, but we lack the confidence to take risk. Disclosure of controversial positions is rare since on this rung we fear others' judgment. Not much gets accomplished.

Eventually, a natural risk-taker gets antsy with all the surface-level courtesy and urges the group to get real. Now we're in motion and we move up to the ***Why Are We Here?*** rung. Here we set goals, put some essential items on the table, and take baby steps in transparency. Some of our hidden thoughts emerge, but factions begin to form. Many feel like uncommitted individuals, not team members.

Next is the ***Bid for Power*** rung. Factions assume more influence. Win/lose interactions are frequent. More opinions are voiced; healthy engagement is growing. But because emotions run high, creative ideas can fall flat. Many groups get stuck here. We get to keep climbing if we overcome our challenges *together.*

Constructive is next. Having found ways to safely disagree and solve problems without power moves, we begin putting the team before our own interests. Factions dissolve, attitudes improve, and team spirit builds. Conflict is now seen as positive. Leadership is shared, and active listening prevails. It's fun!

The highest rung is ***Esprit de Corps,*** where energy flows rapidly among a highly cohesive, trusting team. All are accepted for who we are, and we love being together. There's such intense loyalty to the group that introducing new members now causes reversion to a lower rung. It's the golden stage, and often fleeting.

Today, I will take an honest look at how my family, team, or business is behaving. By knowing where I am, I can make a plan to get where I want to go.

DAY 55: JAIL

We notice ourselves in a shaky trust situation. Our natural fight-or-flight response is twitching, but we feel locked into a condition or pattern of behavior like we're serving out a prison sentence. We need a way forward—now!

At this point in thought or emotion, what we need—viable options to consider—eludes us.

Even when our current views seem justified, I often coach people to *purposely suspend* or *soften* them. Our rigid mindset is possibly in our way.

Try this out: "The consequences here are important. So how can I nudge this relationship in a better direction, assuming that this person is, like me, *reluctant but willing to budge* under the right conditions?"

We may not know what to do, but at least now we are free to brainstorm a list of ideas. We might try:

- Avoiding texts and email. Call, or even better, talk face-to-face.

- Showing vulnerability with "I" statements. "I'm frustrated that we don't seem to communicate well together" (See Day 38, *You, We, and I*).
- Asking open-ended questions such as, "What do you think about _____?" or, "When _____ happens between us, how do you feel?"
- Responding to what they say instead of competing over who's right.
- Exploring a new set of targets and measures to enhance our teamwork.
- Showing our interdependence in some way, by asking for their help.
- Ending the relationship, if necessary (See Day 48, *The Popeye Moment*).

The point, of course, is that we do ourselves a big disservice by surrendering to our feelings of being stuck in jail. It's a lie. As long as we knead this dough in our heads, we remain blind to the many options we have available.

Today I will ask myself where I feel stuck in my trust relationships. By letting go of my own rigid thoughts and beliefs, I have the key to unlock the door.

DAY 56: MAGIC WORDS AND MONKEYS

Can there be trust without accountability? Unlikely. Day 9, *Good Intentions,* focuses on why our good intentions are not enough. Today we tackle the art of holding *others* to account. We trust those who are answerable for their commitments, so tackling accountability is a skill we need.

For accountability to take hold, one must acknowledge that they are responsible for something: the monkey is on their back for it. So "I'll do my best" or "I'll try" do not qualify. Once a firm commitment is made, accountability is straightforward.

A powerful habit is to never ask why a task is incomplete. That's not your business unless you want their monkey to jump to you. Instead ask: "What's your next step to get that done?" Followed by, "When will it happen?" Wait for a new commitment. Then say the magic words: "Can I count on you for that?"

Almost everyone responds well to this. You'll both have cleared up future accountability.

Remember a simple truth: *whoever makes the decision is accountable.* If you make a choice, you are accountable; if they do, they are. If you say, "I can't accept this performance," the monkey just jumped. A better approach: "Do you agree that this performance is not okay? Thanks for taking responsibility. So where do we go from here?" Now, wait for their answer. Their monkey remains where it belongs.

Quick story. I trusted my daughter Kelly to go out in the evenings with her high school friends, but I had to wake up early to leave for work. My need to know she was home by her curfew conflicted with my need for sleep! We both had accountabilities here, right? Hers was to be home on time. Mine was to be a responsible dad. Our solution? Set a loud alarm outside my bedroom door. Kelly's job was to get home to turn it off. If the bell sounded, I knew there was a problem, got up, and dealt with it. If not, it was sweet dreams for me, and a happy, reliable teenager was now home in bed. Both monkeys stayed put!

Today, since I don't want a trust problem to grow, I will respect another person enough to hold them accountable. They get to keep their own monkeys.

DAY 57: GUARDRAILS

Many of us struggle with transparency, with sharing our full opinions. On Day 5, *Just Say It*, we discuss why this can interfere with would-be trust-builders. Today we look at the opposite: the equally unhelpful notion that to be authentic, we need to (or indeed, have a license to) share just about every thought that enters our minds. Do you know someone like this? Is it you?

The reasoning goes: if I hold something back, I'm being dishonest or deceptive, and that's not okay with me. I care too much for another person or my own integrity to tolerate this. They deserve to know what I think and feel. I have to be me. Or else it's all a lie. *If what I say troubles you, I'm sorry, but that's just me being me.*

Being with someone who discloses every thought as it comes feels much like a passenger on a narrow mountain road without guardrails. We welcome the exhilaration and unique experience of such flagrant exposure, but we can't relax. We stay vigilant and look ahead to see where this might go, knowing that we can't hit the brakes if needed. Their genuineness is refreshing, but it's scary and exhausting, too.

As I've said many times, once trust is well-established between two people, there can be a relaxation of discipline. Things flow easily and naturally, without as much introspection. In fact, this is an excellent sign of trust.

But there should never be a point at which either member of the relationship forgets their responsibility to provide safety for the other. If what you are about to say is accusatory, scary, insensitive, or could trigger your trusting partner, you owe it to them and yourself to pause. Recast what you're about to say in a safe manner that allows them to constructively absorb it. This is not deception; it's caring.

Today I will ask myself whether the people in the relationships I am building need to know every thought that runs through my head. My desire for authenticity does not override their need for a safe, reasonable pace up the trust mountain.

DAY 58: COME ON DOWN

Many of us would-be trust-builders have a blind spot with our humility. That is, we like to think we treat everyone with equal care and concern, but too often this just isn't the case.

Internally, we can compare ourselves against other people, seeking ways we might have an advantage. For example, we might look at ourselves and think, "I have more experience, more responsibility, more money, better looks, or a better grasp on reality than this other person." Or we think, "They have less than I do in one or more of these areas." When seeing them this way, how humble are we?

Anything that distances us from other people is a direct blow to our ability to connect with them on a human level. And regarding trust, this is what matters—not that other stuff. People don't trust those who look down on them. They can't afford it.

If we believe we are somehow better than the person with whom we're attempting to build trust, then we are fooling ourselves—on both counts. Our nonverbal signals, which they will pick up, will reinforce this belief and block the trust we hope to build. The fact is we aren't better, merely different. Genuine trust-builders must come down off self-constructed pedestals so we can relate, listen to, and connect with fellow human beings who are no better or worse than we are.

This sounds like such a simple thing. It isn't. It sets apart those who see trust as its own reward from those who want the *outcomes* of extraordinary trust. The more we practice seeing everyone as equals, the easier it becomes. Just don't let this get to your head, though, or you'll have to start all over.

Today I will keep in mind that I'm no better or worse than anybody else. Knowing this, I can approach each person on equal footing—relating to them as the valuable, unique people they are. As I do, they will know they can trust me.

DAY 59: THE MIRAGE

Fearless trust-building: it doesn't exist.

Many spouses, parents, and leaders feel relieved with the absence of conflict. Given the pressures hitting us from all sides, the relative quiet of people "getting along" can be like an oasis in the desert. If only it would last.

Genuine high-trust environments are found well beyond the comfort zone. And there's precisely one way to get there: by diving into uncomfortable topics, listening fully to other peoples' viewpoints, and *sacrificing* getting along in favor of vulnerable candor.

While every relationship or group is unique, many people tend to silently and repeatedly accept behaviors that erode their trust. We continue to wear smiles in our interactions while mistrust takes root. Eventually, the fear of confrontation takes over and we get stuck in the pattern. In retrospect, we chose to get along instead of using the problem as an opportunity to build trust. This is an observation, not an accusation.

Is our getting along a mirage that's keeping us from facing underlying challenges? Every team, marriage, and relationship needs an occasional spring cleaning. And if the calendar didn't tell us to, many of us wouldn't do it.

It's why I recommend we periodically answer the following questions, alone, and then review them together as a trust-building exercise:

- In my mind, what thoughts am I paying rent to that I haven't shared with my spouse/friend/teammate(s)?
- What do I believe but I've been afraid to say aloud?
- I haven't shared my concern(s) so far because...
- What, if anything, could help me feel safer in this relationship or group?

Today I will distinguish between getting along and real trust, which is what I want.

DAY 60: BUT I HAVE TRUST ISSUES

We will encounter people who do not respond to our best attempts to build trust. They may even warn us: "Hey, don't take it personally; I don't trust anyone." What is a trust-builder to do in this case? Give up? Push harder?

Let's back up a minute. First, someone who says this rarely does so frivolously, so we've just been given significant, even revealing, information. We don't know—and may never learn—why they have difficulty trusting, but we do know they've been through the wringer somewhere in the past.

It's a good bet that multiple people, over extended periods, have withdrawn this person's trust. If they were young when this happened, it likely affected their ability to trust themselves as well. Being let down, by self and others, can become a lifelong pattern—to the point where the safest road, but not the happiest, is to trust nobody.

It's a lonely path, but there's hope. I know because this was my story. (My first book, *On My Own, Recollections of an Unlikely CEO*, shares my boyhood isolation and why trust now means so much to me.)

It's this understanding that holds the key to our trust-building approach. No matter who we are or what our role is, we cannot fix this problem. Nor can we force this person to trust us. We can't even convince them with reason. The best approach to build trust with a low-trusting person is to be kind, consistent, and to keep the door open.

Often, in truth, this person can be a lonely soul, seeking to connect with safe people, but afraid to admit it—even to themselves. There's a good reason we want this person's trust. These folks are often the most loyal people we'll ever know. But we need to bring our A-game. And stay with it.

Today I will respect another person's difficulty in trusting me or anyone else. I don't have to fix, force, or convince them that I am trustworthy. I choose kindness and will leave my door open for them to enter when they're good and ready.

COOL DOWN
(CONCLUSION)

Congratulations! You made it through the Building Trust 60-Day Workout. You are now much more sensitive to the impact you have on the relationships in your life.

Keep this little book handy for when your significant dealings with others need some fresh oil. The Index can help you target topics of particular interest.

It's important to remember that no one works the trust-building skills perfectly, and neither will you. Or me. But take heart. We, humans, are a forgiving lot. If people recognize sincere effort on our part to be genuine, reliable, and true to our word, then they are likely to overlook occasional mistakes along the way.

Like all workouts, repetition and commitment bring results. If this was your first trip through the book, research shows that within two weeks,

80 percent of what you just read will be forgotten. Therefore, mark your calendar today to pick this up again in six months. Reread those pages that stick out to you as particularly interesting, either because they identified your strengths or shed light on a blind spot.

If you enjoyed this experience, I encourage you to follow Building Trust, LLC on social media (Twitter, Facebook, Instagram, and LinkedIn) to keep up with our continuing writings and other developments in the world of practical trust-building.

Building Trust, founded in 2008, offers four service pathways to our clients:

- The Building Trust Experience, a highly interactive two-day workshop
- Team training and development, for workgroups seeking a breakthrough
- Professional leadership coaching, in a private, one-to-one environment
- Custom one-time events of all kinds (keynotes, special sessions, etc.)

To learn more or reserve time for an exploratory conversation, contact **bruce@brucehendrick.com**.

EPILOGUE

As I said in my first book, the memoir *On My Own, Recollections of an Unlikely CEO*, uncovering my personal WHY—my purpose and passion—was pivotal. The more I live according to my WHY, the more energetic and joyous I feel.

My personal WHY: *To be authentically myself, to help bring order to chaotic situations, to establish trust in all my relationships, and to arm others to reduce their isolation in life and career.*

To be authentically myself was hazardous as a youngster, and now I take immense pleasure in the simple act of following my own compass. As a leader, authenticity—even when it means not looking presidential—allows me to make real connections with real people. Plus, it's a lot easier than faking it.

To help bring order to chaotic situations was a required skill in our family. To my surprise, I have discovered that I don't want to "get over" this. The knack of keeping a cool head, quickly diagnosing a problem, and taking decisive action turns out to be highly valued both at home and in the workplace.

To establish trust in all my relationships is a life-long desire. I can think of no higher compliment than for two people to honestly say, "I can count on you." Considering where I started, having a large pool of mutually trusting relationships means the world to me.

To arm others to reduce their isolation in life and career may be the most compelling part of my WHY. I know what it feels like to be alone, and I am driven to do whatever I can to relieve others of this burden while I'm still here. It's the reason I founded Building Trust and wrote this book.

IF I'VE BUILT TRUST WITH YOU...

Then you may decide to consider the services of Building Trust, LLC for yourself or your organization.

Take another quick look at Day 27, *The Price Tag*. Calculate the costs of the elements that surround you today. If you're unwilling to continue to pay this bill, we can help. Plus, think about the initiatives you have on your horizon. How would greatly enhanced organizational trust make them go better, faster, farther, and with less stress?

The Building Trust Proven Process

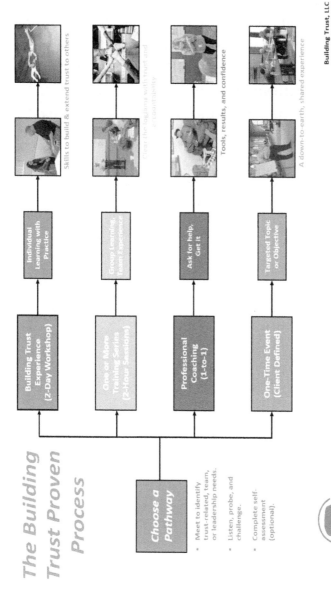

Choose a Pathway

- Meet to identify trust-related, team, or leadership needs.
- Listen, probe, and challenge.
- Complete self-assessment (optional).

Building Trust Experience (2-Day Workshop) → **Individual Learning with Practice**

Skills to build & extend trust to others

One or More Training Series (2-Hour Sessions) → **Group Learning, Team Experience**

Clear challenges with trust and accountability

Professional Coaching (1-to-1) → **Ask for help, Get it**

Tools, results, and confidence

One-Time Event (Client Defined) → **Targeted Topic or Objective**

A down-to-earth, shared experience

*For leaders who are fed up with their team's plateaued performance, we infuse disciplines to **build trust** and take you and your team to a whole new place.*

Building Trust, LLC
330-601-0898
www.brucehendrick.com
carrie@brucehendrick.com
bruce@brucehendrick.com

BruceHendrick
BUILDING TRUST

Each daily lesson in this workout deserves further treatment, more in-depth discussion, and practical training. That's what we're here for.

Visit us at **www.brucehendrick.com** to stay abreast of future opportunities, ask a question, or sign up for our newsletter. Follow us on LinkedIn, Twitter, Facebook, and Instagram.

INDEX

ABOUT THE AUTHOR

Bruce Hendrick founded Building Trust, LLC in 2008 to help professionals in all walks of life become more effective through improving their interpersonal communication, trust-building, and leadership skills. He offers many services along these lines and is a popular and sought-after national public speaker.

If you enjoyed reading *The Building Trust 60-Day Workout*, you might also enjoy Bruce's first book, *On My Own, Recollections of an Unlikely CEO,* which tells the compelling story of Bruce's childhood family as it wrestled with the consequences of mental illness.

Bruce also serves as the owner and CEO of RBB, The Small Batch Experts, a 55-person electronics assembly company in Wooster, Ohio. RBB has been serving the custom electronics needs of the industrial and medical marketplace since 1973. To learn more about RBB, visit **www.rbbsystems.com**.

On the road to his RBB role, he led everything from Boy Scout peers to night shifts at fast food joints to significant change efforts in Fortune 500 companies. His down-to-earth style is always based on what works with real people in the real world.

Made in the USA
Coppell, TX
16 September 2021

62507862R00089